wee felt WORLDS

wee felt WORLDS

Sweet Little Scenes to Needle Felt

edited by
Amanda Carestio

LARK CRAFTS

Asheville

Development Editor:
Thom O'Hearn

Editorial Intern:
Alex Alesi

Art Director:
Shannon Yokeley

Illustrator:
Orrin Lundgren

Photographer:
Steve Mann

Cover Designer:
Shannon Yokeley

LARK CRAFTS

An Imprint of Sterling Publishing
387 Park Avenue South
New York, NY 10016

If you have questions or comments about
this book, please visit: larkcrafts.com

Library of Congress Cataloging-in-Publication Data

Wee felt worlds : sweet little scenes to needle felt / edited by Amanda Carestio.
-- First Edition.
    pages cm
  Includes index.
  ISBN 978-1-4547-0393-8 (pbk. : alk. paper)
  1. Felt work. 2. Soft sculpture. I. Carestio, Amanda.
  TT849.5.W44 2013
  746'.0463--dc23
                                2012018294

10 9 8 7 6 5 4 3 2 1

First Edition

Published by Lark Crafts
An Imprint of Sterling Publishing Co., Inc.
387 Park Avenue South, New York, NY 10016

© 2013, Lark Crafts, an Imprint of Sterling Publishing Co., Inc.

Distributed in Canada by Sterling Publishing,
c/o Canadian Manda Group, 165 Dufferin Street
Toronto, Ontario, Canada M6K 3H6

Distributed in the United Kingdom by GMC Distribution Services,
Castle Place, 166 High Street, Lewes, East Sussex, England BN7 1XU

Distributed in Australia by Capricorn Link (Australia) Pty Ltd.,
P.O. Box 704, Windsor, NSW 2756 Australia

Manufactured in China

ISBN 13: 978-1-4547-0393-8

For information about custom editions, special sales, and premium
and corporate purchases, please contact Sterling Special Sales
Department at 800-805-5489 or specialsales@sterlingpub.com.

Requests for information about desk and examination copies
available to college and university professors must be submitted
to academic@larkbooks.com. Our complete policy can be found
at www.larkcrafts.com.

contents

Welcome, friends!

Welcome to our Wee Felt World!

There's something so magical about things made in miniature. How about creating a whole wee world of them? You can … with needle felting.

Creating three-dimensional critters—and snowmen and pine trees and carnivorous plants—is easy with needle felting. Essentially a kind of dry felting, the process is quite basic and requires only a few tools.

Here's how it works: during the dry-felting process, you'll use a felting needle to penetrate wool roving repeatedly to create specific forms. Barbs on the needle latch onto the felt, tangling and enmeshing the layers to create a firm shape. And that's really about as complicated as it gets! If you're new to needle felting, though, take a look at the Getting Started section. It'll tell you what you need, teach you the basic techniques, and get your creative (felt!) juices flowing.

From there, the possibilities are endless. Try these wee worlds on for size:

LITTLE CUB'S ADVENTURE (page 16) includes a cute bear cub, his trusty canine sidekick, a steaming cup of cocoa, a pine tree, and a roaring fire.

SWEET SHOPPE (page 68) features all things sweet, delicious, and felty: handmade truffles, too-cute cupcakes, donuts (complete with felted sprinkles!), delectable ice pops, and lollipops so real you'll be tempted to give them a lick!

LAND OF THE DINOSAURS (page 32) showcases a pair of majestic (felt!) dinosaurs, complete with foliage, spotted eggs, and a dino fossil to complete the prehistoric scene.

CIRCUS MAXIMUS (page 58) presents a dapper ringmaster, a lion strongman, and a fire-breathing elephant…. Step right up for the show!

AND MANY MORE SCENES, ALL CREATED BY A TALENTED GROUP OF DESIGNERS!

They've also included loads of tips and techniques along the way: ideas for creating armatures, info on making secure joints, and all kinds of tricks for shaping felt. You'll be ready to branch out with your own needle-felt creations in no time.

And we just couldn't help ourselves. We were so inspired by the imaginative scenes each designer created, that we had to mix-and-match our own. Take a quick peek at page 122—we had fun and we hope it shows! It's kind of hard not to with this kind of cuteness!

So get started, go forth, and create a new felt world!

Getting Started with Needle Felting

Even if you've never needle felted before, you can get started rather quickly. The techniques in this book focus largely on three-dimensional objects created by dry felting with a needle or needles. Here's a rundown of the materials you'll gather, the tools you'll use, and the techniques you'll need to create the projects in this book.

The Materials

You don't need much to create a world all your own: just some wool roving, a felting needle, and a work surface.

Wool Roving

Essentially carded wool drawn into long continuous strands, wool roving is available online and in small and large craft stores alike in a myriad of colors, and it's a good thing! As a general guide, medium to coarse wools work best for needle felting.

When you're getting ready to use or parcel out a chunk of roving, simply pull an amount off the end of the strand; don't use your scissors to cut it. Use the photo below as a guide when pulling out wool roving. We've used the same scale for the projects in this book.

Unless otherwise indicated, all of the projects in this book use less than ¼ ounce (7 grams) of roving in any given color, and many use much, much less. If you need more than that amount—say, for the charming, but rather large T-Rex on page 34—we've indicated the amount of roving required. You'll soon learn, though, that working with roving amounts is not an exact science: a lot depends on how you work, what base material you're using if any (especially if you're using a different technique than the ones recommended in the project instructions), and the kind of coverage you like to have in your projects. But this chart should be helpful!

¼ ounce (7 grams) = about the size of a peach

½ ounce (14 grams) = about the size of an apple

1 ounce (28 grams) = about the size of a grapefruit

1½ ounces (43 grams) = about the size of a melon

2 ounces (57 grams) = about the size of a squash

Precut polystyrene foam is another great option for a needle-felting base. Simply use a precut shape or cut a piece to your needed dimensions and then needle felt on a layer of roving.

When it comes to giving your creatures shape—and a pose-able shape at that!—chenille stems (aka pipe cleaners) are your friend. Chenille stems are perfect for arms, stalks, legs, and other limbs.

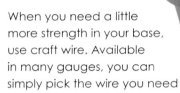

When you need a little more strength in your base, use craft wire. Available in many gauges, you can simply pick the wire you need for the task at hand. The project instructions will specify what gauge or thickness to use. To work with this kind of wire, you'll need needle-nose pliers and wire cutters on hand.

Embellishments
What would a wee felt world be without embellishments! The projects in this book use a variety of extras, some of which serve a specific purpose and some of which are merely for (super cute!) decoration. Yarn, beads, buttons, and embroidery floss (as in Wooly Woodland, page 92) are all perfect for creating eyes, mouths, faces, and little design details.

The Tools
You actually need very little in the way of tools for successful needle felting.

Needles
Before we go any further into the various types and sizes of needles, a word of caution: These needles are very sharp! Keep them away from children and use caution as you work, especially when you're holding a 3-D object, as the needles are long and

Craft Felt
Many of the projects in this book also involve a bit of craft felt together with wool roving. You can needle felt roving directly onto craft felt or use the craft felt as a design element, especially when you need a thin layer (as for leaves or foliage) or a very precise shape. With the proper amount of needle felting, many types of craft felt will work with roving, though wool felt sheets seems to work the best. Craft felt is available in sheets or off the bolt, both online and in a variety of craft stores.

For the craft felt pieces in many of the projects, there are templates in the back of the book. Simply enlarge the templates to the size indicated, pin or trace the shapes on your felt, and cut the number of shapes you need for the project.

Supports & Substrates
Wool roving, in and of itself, doesn't have much form or shape. As you start to needle felt it, it will firm up, but sometimes it's best to start with a material for the base of the shape you're creating, especially when you're working on a larger shape.

In many of the projects in this book, plain wool roving or stuffing is used to create the base shape, which is then covered with a layer of colored roving. Going this route makes a lot of sense: why waste all those lovely colors where they won't show!

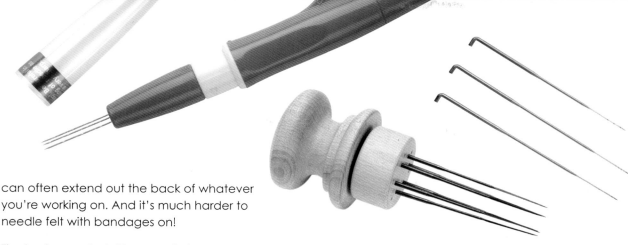

can often extend out the back of whatever you're working on. And it's much harder to needle felt with bandages on!

The basic needle-felting needle is about 3½ to 4 inches (8.9 to 10.2 cm) long and made of steel. These needles have a super sharp point and little barbs along the edges, which do the actual felting, or blending of layers. Needles come in different sizes and shapes, based on the task at hand, though I've found that triangular needles work best for multiple tasks. The size is indicated by number; the higher the number, the finer the needle. Again, I've got a favorite here for general tasks—size 38—but here's a brief rundown of the other sizes available.

40 – fine, perfect for small details
38 – a good standard size
36 – good for coarse wool and general shaping

Some designers indicate which needles to use for which projects and tasks; others do not. As you work, you'll quickly come to find what works best for you. And until then, rest assured: It's really not an exact science!

If you're covering a large area, try using a multi-needle tool. Try one of the slick, pen-like tools that are on the market now. These usually hold three or four needles, and they're really easy to hold and use. Capable of holding even more needles is the wooden-handled multi-needle tool, perfect for quick felting—you can really cover a lot of ground with this tool! In both cases, the needles can be switched in and out, should you have a needle break or prefer to change sizes. There are even needle-felting machines, which look like sewing machines with multiple needles, though these are best-suited for large, flat surfaces.

Work Surface

A word to the wise: do not needle felt on your favorite craft table unless you like the Swiss cheese look (and broken needles to boot)!

There are special foam surfaces just for needle felting, but I've found that dense upholstery foam—about 2 inches (5.1 cm) thick—works wonderfully well. As you work, the foam supports your piece and keeps your needles from damaging the surface underneath (and from breaking). You can get pretty far with just a single block of foam, but eventually you'll need to replace it, as the fibers break down.

Other Tools

You'll need a few other handy tools for the projects in this book, but you've likely already got these around the house: scissors, sewing needles, and needle-nose pliers and wire cutters, if you're working with wire armatures.

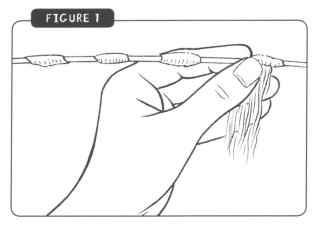

FIGURE 1

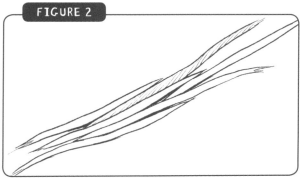

FIGURE 2

Invasion of the Dioramas

Use the scenes in this book to create your own fun dioramas, or mix-and-match the elements if the mood strikes you. What if your T-rex has a sweet tooth and sneaks into the sweet shoppe for a donut? And the space aliens decide to take a vacation to prehistoric Earth? It's crossover time! Let your felt creatures have fun in each other's worlds. We sure did, and you can see the results in the back of the book on page 122.

The Techniques

As you'll soon discover, needle felting—and especially dry felting—is a very forgiving craft. Added a detail that's not quite right? Simply pull it off and start again. Is your base shape not shaping up? Add more felt and continue felting. With dry felting, the process is essentially the same, no matter what task you're performing. Simply insert the needle straight down into the felt layers and then withdraw from the same hole, working in a straight up-and-down motion. Move around as you work to create an even surface. As you move the needle in and out of the felt, the barbs catch and drop the felt fibers, tangling and enmeshing the layers to create a firm shape. From here, we'll cover a few specific techniques for shaping, creating joints, and working with felt.

Creating Basic Shapes

Remember working with clay as a kid? Felt roving works on many of the same principles!

To create spheres: For small spheres—like eyeballs—simply grab a small chunk of roving and roll it between your palms, working in multiple directions. For larger spheres, spin the roving onto a dowel or skewer (fig. 1), then pull the felt off the dowel. Needle felt your sphere until firm. This technique was used in a number of projects.

To create chains: Simply roll the felt between your palms, working in a side-to-side motion, until your chain is the length and width you'd like it to be (fig. 2).

To create a hollow shape: Roll the roving around a tool—like a pen—and needle felt (fig. 3) as you continue to add felt. Remove the shape and felt until firm. This technique is particularly handy for donut making (page 74)!

To create a detailed shape: While there are special needle-felting molds and stencils on the market, you can also put your baking supplies to good use for felting shapes. Position a cookie cutter on your work surface, place a chunk of roving inside the shape, and felt straight down into the shape (taking care not to hit the sides of the cutter) (fig. 4). Continue adding felt and felting until the shape is the thickness you'd like, and don't forget the backside!

TIP: *Since most of these projects involve three-dimensional shapes, you'll need to keep each side of the shape in mind as you work. Turn your piece often to check that all sides are neat and tidy.*

Working with Base Materials & Supports

If you're making a big shape or a shape with, say, appendages, it's a good idea to start with an underlying base structure to give your project form and, in some cases, function.

Core wool

Particularly helpful if you're working on a large scale (like the Stegosaurus on page 38), core wool, wool stuffing, or fiberfill can be used to create the base for your shape (fig. 5). Once you've got the basic shapes constructed, cover the base material with colored roving.

Foam

Perfect when you're working to create a large, well-defined shape, polystyrene foam makes a sturdy base for needle felting, and it's available in a number of handy pre-cut shapes, like the cone used for the Pine Tree (page 23). If you're handy with a knife, you could also cut your own base shape from the foam. Then simply wrap the roving around the shape and needle felt it in place. If you'd like a softer feel, you can also use upholstery foam as a base.

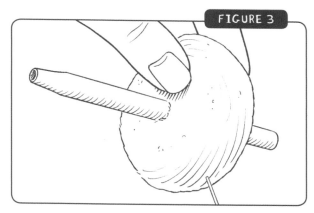
FIGURE 3

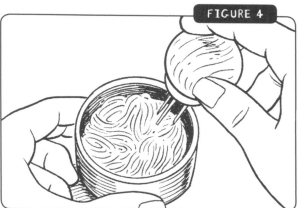
FIGURE 4

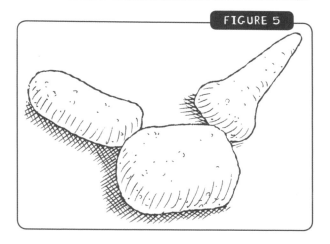
FIGURE 5

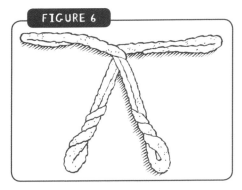

FIGURE 6

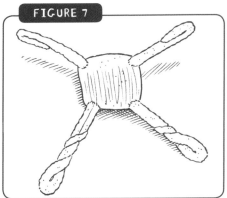

FIGURE 7

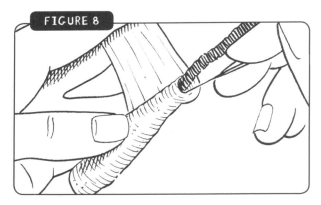

FIGURE 8

Armatures

If you need to create posable limbs, branches, or other features that can hold their shape, armatures make a useful base for needle felting. For the projects in this book, we used two main kinds of armatures: chenille stems and thick-gauge craft wire.

Finally … more useful uses for chenille stems! They're perfect for building shape under your wool roving, and the roving clings nicely to the velvety fibers. Simply create the base shape with the chenille stems, wrap a bit of felt around the shape, and continue wrapping around the extremities (figs. 6–8). Do take care when you're felting roving onto these stems though: Steer clear of the wire as you work or you'll risk breaking your needle.

For something that needs to hold a bit more weight, try thick-gauge craft wire. It's a bit harder to needle felt roving directly to this wire, so your best bet is to cover the wire with a layer of craft felt, and then build outward. Start at the bottom with a nice coil wrap (fig. 9). Then wrap craft felt around the shape and secure with glue (fig. 10). For lighter support, like foliage, you can also use a lighter gauge wire, whatever is strong enough to support the felt you're about to attach.

From Wee Felt World to Real World

The projects in this book don't have to sit still once they're finished. They can be used for all kinds of things! Small felt objects work great as jewelry: the wee mushrooms may look perfect as part of Wooly Woodlands, but they'd also make sweet earrings. Attach a magnet to one of the Sweet Shoppe donuts for cute refrigerator décor, or replace the fuzzy dice under your rearview mirror with a UFO. The T-Rex and Stegosaurus make irresistible toys for kids, and the items from Deck the Halls would make perfect Christmas decorations or ornaments. Your wee felt creations can moonlight as almost anything!

Creating Joints

What's a creature without limbs ... or a T-Rex without tiny arms! Creating joints is an important step for adding limbs to your felt creatures—and other felt shapes—and you've got options.

If you don't need your limbs to move, a solid joint might be all you need. Here, you're simply attaching the limb or part directly to the main body. Hold the limb against the main body and needle felt the shapes together, working from the limb into the body and from the body into the limb (fig. 11). Add a bit of roving around the joint for added security. Continue needle felting until the joint seems solid.

If you'd like moving limbs or parts, choose a string joint. Useful for all kinds of attachments, string joints are just that: joints held together with string and a few sewing stitches. The instructions for each project will provide specifics, but the process is usually quite similar: Knot and stitch from the main body into the limb or part, and stitch back into the main body (fig. 12), repeating until the joint seems solid. Tie off and hide your knot under a bit of roving.

Working with Colors

Think of roving as your paints and your little world, the canvas! Blendable, shade-able, and colorful, felt roving is magical stuff. Here are a few techniques for working with color.

Shading with roving

Shading with felt is easy and fun, and it can provide your project with depth and dimension. To do this effectively, you'll need a few close, gradated shades in the color of your choice. Start felting with one shade (likely either your lightest or your darkest shade), move to the medium shade, and then continue working across the surface of your object, changing shades and working either light to dark (which is probably easier) or dark to light. You can also blend your own gradated shades if you like.

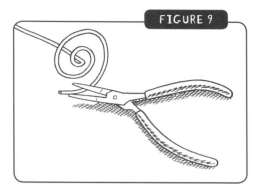

FIGURE 9

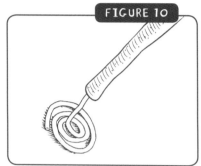

FIGURE 10

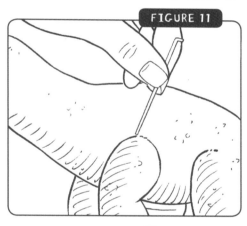

FIGURE 11

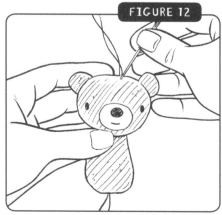

FIGURE 12

Blending colors

Create just the shade you need if you don't have the right one! Simply stack layers of two colors of felt roving, pull the felt apart, restack, and repeat. This will give you a soft, blended, and almost-mottled effect, perfect for natural elements like mushroom tops and animal fur.

Coloring with fabric paint

Got a paintbrush and a bit of fabric paint? Then you can add color to your felt creations easily. Mix your paint with a bit of water for a soft wash effect or leave the colors bright and bold, then just brush it on.

Adding Embellishments

Besides roving, you can add all manner of materials to add details, depth, and texture to your felt world. One of our favorites is—you guessed it!—craft felt. Perfect for creating foliage, critter clothing, and any thin, flat, detailed shapes you need, craft felt can be a lifesaver. To attach it to your creation, you can needle felt it on, stitch it down, or glue it in place. If you're going to needle felt roving directly into craft felt, we've found that wool craft felt is best.

Another handy embellishment is wool yarn, great for creating strong lines and for defining shapes. Simply lay the yarn over your creation and needle felt it in place. If you need a finer line, split the yarn, as you would embroidery floss, before felting it in place.

And the fun doesn't stop there! Use a bit of embroidery floss, a needle, and some simple stitches to create eyes, a mouth, and other details. Or bring in beads (perfect for little eyes) and buttons for added texture.

Other Techniques

While it's nice and romantic to be a purist when it comes to needle felting, we've embraced the glue gun in this book. It's invaluable when you need to secure little bits, for working with craft felt, and for securing felt to base wire. General craft glue also works wonders; just be sure you don't end up with stray globs anywhere.

You can also use glue to sturdy up craft felt, to help it hold a particular shape. Just check out Chrissy Mahuna's Fan Palms, page 45. Mix a bit of glue with water, dunk the craft felt in the mixture, mold it into the shape you'd like, and then let it dry.

Setting the Stage

Every scene needs a stage. Show off your wee felt creations by building a display. You can go simple—think found teacups or bowls, wood bases, or shelves—or get creative and build something that looks to have come straight out of your felt world! A terrarium might be perfect for your prehistoric friends from Land of the Dinosaurs, while the starfish, seaweed, and crab from Pirate Island might feel at home in a fish bowl. Redub the bowl a "space helmet" to accommodate the cast of The Felt Galaxy ... and Beyond. Show off your work, and give your creations their own place to live!

Who lives in your wee felt world?

Little Cub's
ADVENTURE

Have you packed your felt marshmallows? Check. Hot cocoa? Check. Camping companion? Of course! Then you're ready to set out for the great (felt!) outdoors.

Created by Jenn Docherty

Little Bear

This cute cub is fully string jointed, so you can pose him by his campfire any which way you like.

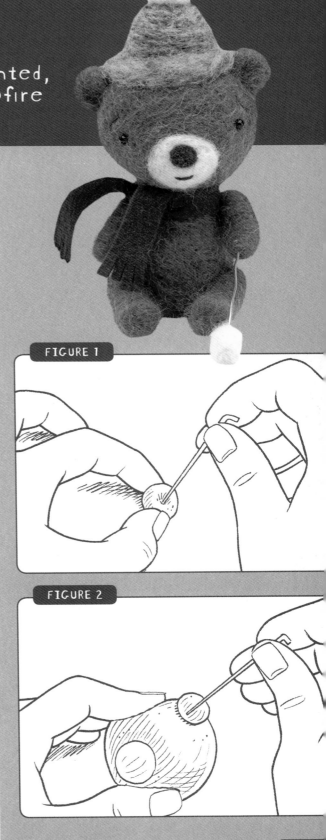

Finished Size
4 inches (10.2 cm) tall

Materials & Tools
Felting needle
Foam felting mat
Wool stuffing for core
Brown, white, dark brown, and turquoise roving
Brown craft felt
Wooden skewer
Black beads
Sewing needle and brown thread
Fine gauge wire
Long sewing needle
Upholstery thread
Glue

1 Tightly roll a palm-sized tuft of wool stuffing into an egg shape to create the **HEAD**. Place the shape on a foam mat, and needle felt until it's reduced in size and firmly felted.

2 Cover the core with a layer of brown roving and felt it into place.

3 To make the **SNOUT**, felt a small tuft of brown roving onto the center of the head. Continue to felt until it is smooth and seamless. Add more roving if necessary. Felt a small tuft of white roving onto the snout.

4 To make the **EARS**, roll a small bit of roving into a ball and felt it until firm. Concentrate your felting onto the center of ball to make an indentation (fig. 1). Needle felt the ear to the head (fig. 2).

5 To make the **BODY**, roll a tuft of wool stuffing into a cylinder and felt it until moderately firm. Concentrate your felting on one end of the body, creating a torso and a belly. Cover the body with brown roving. Add more roving to the belly area as necessary to create a round tummy.

FIGURE 1

FIGURE 2

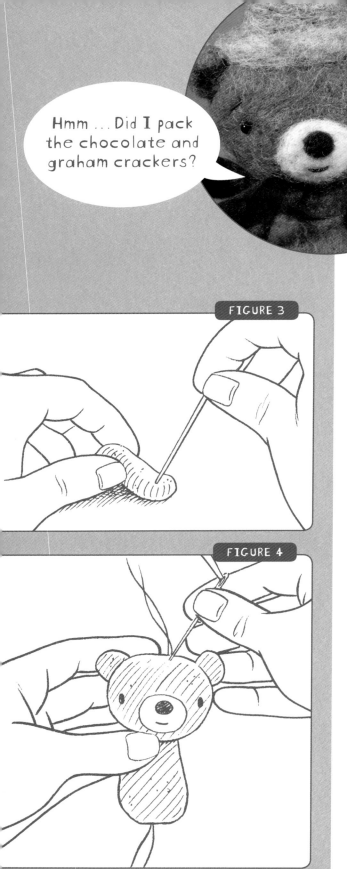

Hmm ... Did I pack the chocolate and graham crackers?

FIGURE 3

FIGURE 4

6 To make the **LEGS**, pull two evenly sized tufts of roving. Fold these in half and begin felting on the folded end to create the upper leg. Fold over the wispy end and felt to create the bottom of the leg (fig. 3). Add a small ball of roving to the leg and shape it to create a **FOOT**.

7 To make the **ARMS**, wrap roving around a wooden skewer, and twirl it between your fingers until secure. Slide the arm off of the skewer, and felt the ends until rounded. Focus your felting to create an indentation for the crook of arm.

8 Felt a small dark brown tuft of roving onto the snout to create a **NOSE**. Attach beads for eyes and sew small stitches to create the mouth and eyebrows.

9 Assemble the bear. Thread thin gauge wire through a long needle and enter through the bottom of body, up through the head, and back down, two times, ending at the bottom (fig. 4). Twist the wire to secure and snip and coil up to hide it.

10 Attach the arms and legs. Thread a length of upholstery thread through the inside of one arm, and tie a knot. Sew through the body and tie off. Thread through the inside of the other arm and down through the body to the location of the leg joint. Repeat, as with the arms, to attach the legs. Exit through the bottom of body and tie off. Cover the wire and thread at the bottom with a small tuft of roving.

11 To make the **HAT**, felt a tuft of turquoise wool into a cone shape, keeping the bottom wide and concentrating felting on the top to create a narrow point. Felt the hat to the head. Felt a small ball of white roving to top of the hat.

12 To make the **SCARF**, cut a long thin strip of brown felt and tie it around the neck.

13 To make the **MARSHMALLOW**, felt a small ball of white roving. Felt the ends until they're flattened. Using the upholstery needle, poke a hole into one end of the marshmallow. Dab a small bit of glue on the end of the wire, and poke it into the hole. Poke another hole in end of bear's hand, and glue the other end of the wire into the hand.

Doggie

This little guy is the perfect wee companion for any camping adventure; just make sure you pack extra felt marshmallows for him!

Finished Size
1¾ x 1¼ inches (4.4 x 3.2 cm)

Materials & Tools
Felting needle
Foam felting mat
White and brown roving
Wooden skewer
Upholstery thread
Small black beads
Brown thread
Scrap of fabric for neckerchief

1 Create the **BODY** by rolling a tuft of white roving into a small egg shape and felting it until firm.

2 Create the **LEGS** by twirling four evenly sized tufts of white roving onto a wooden skewer and spinning them between your fingers until the fibers begin to adhere (fig. 1). Slide the legs off the skewer.

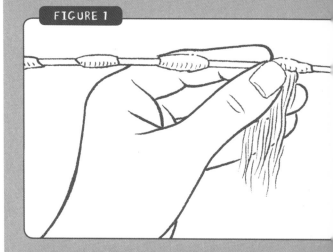

FIGURE 1

Um ... Did you guys hear something?

FIGURE 2

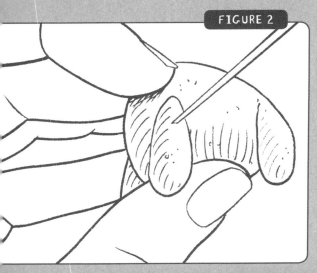

3 Felt one end of each leg, rounding to create a foot. Leave the fibers of the other end loose. Attach each leg by felting the loose fibers to the body (fig. 2).

4 Where the legs attach to the body, place tufts of roving, and felt to smooth out any lumps and bumps, creating an even, uniform look. Use the same method to create and attach a **TAIL**.

5 To make the **HEAD**, roll a tuft of wool roving into a small egg shape. Felt it until firm. Focus your felting on one end of head to create an indentation for the snout.

FIGURE 3

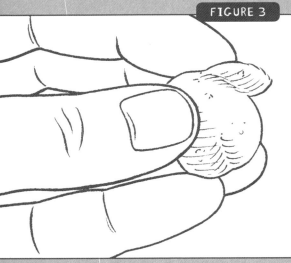

6 To make **EARS**, roll a tiny tuft of white roving between your fingers and felt it into a small teardrop shape, leaving some loose fibers to use to attach to the head. Repeat, making the other ear brown. Felt the ears to head (fig. 3).

7 Attach the head to the body using white upholstery thread. Knot off at the bottom of the body, and hide the excess thread by felting on small tufts of wool.

8 Felt on a small brown **NOSE** and a **SPOT** on the dog's side. Create eyebrows and some whiskers with small stitching using brown thread, and sew on the beads for eyes. Tie a small triangle of fabric around the neck to create a neckerchief.

Cup of Cocoa

A cozy cup of cocoa – with a tiny wisp of white roving steam – is just the thing to warm up your little furry camper.

Finished Size
1½ inches (3.8 cm) tall

Materials & Tools
Felting needle
Foam felting mat
Red, brown, and white roving
Wooden skewer

1 To make the **CUP**, roll red roving around a wooden skewer to create a fat, short cylinder. Spin the shape between your fingers until the fibers adhere. Slide the cylinder off the skewer. Felt the ends until flat.

2 Add **COCOA** by felting on a small circle of brown wool roving onto one end of the cylinder.

3 Attach a small ball of red roving to the side of the cup to form the **HANDLE**. Concentrate your felting in the center of ball to create a handle shape.

4 Add a wispy tuft of white roving to top of the cup to create a bit of **STEAM**.

Fire Pit

Complete with a stone border, this charming little fire pit is really rather convincing.

FIGURE 1

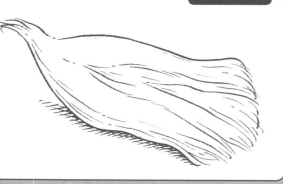

FIGURE 2

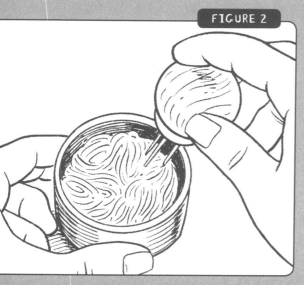

Finished Size
2½ x 4½ inches (6.4 x 11.4 cm)

Materials & Tools
Felting needle
Foam felting mat
Light orange, dark orange, white, brown, and various gray wool roving
2½-inch (6.4 cm) round cookie cutter
Multi-needle tool

1 To create the **FLAMES**, layer a small tuft of white roving, a medium tuft of light orange, and a large tuft of dark orange. Fold the layers in half (fig. 1).

2 Hold the tufts upright on the foam mat, with the folded side down, and felt the bottom to create a base, pressing down and compressing. Gently felt the flames.

3 To create the bottom of **FIRE PIT**, place a tuft of brown roving inside the cookie cutter on top of your foam pad. Use the multi-needle tool to firmly felt it (fig. 2). Remove the cutter, peel the circle off the mat, and flip it over. Place the circle back in the cookie cutter and felt the other side.

4 Attach the fire to the base. To create the **STONE BORDER**, roll tufts of gray roving into spheres, and attach them to the brown base, around the base of the fire.

Pine Tree

Using a foam cone as the base, you can quickly felt up a whole pine tree forest.

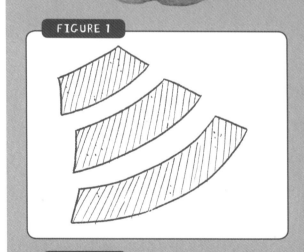

Finished Size
3 x 7 inches (7.6 x 17.8 cm)

Materials & Tools
Felting needle
Foam felting mat
Foam cone
Green wool craft felt
Scissors
Two shades of green roving
Multi-needle felting tool (optional)

1 Make a template by wrapping the wool craft felt around the cone. Trim the excess where the felt overlaps itself. Cut the felt into three curved pieces (fig. 1).

2 Layer a tuft of roving onto the bottom piece of craft felt. Use a multi-needle tool to felt green roving directly onto the craft felt until smooth.

3 Use a single needle to make **SCALLOPS** (fig. 2) by gently pulling the roving into shape with the needle and felting to secure.

4 Wrap the felted shape around the cone and gently felt it in place to secure. Repeat with the other two craft felt pieces.

5 When you attach the top layer, tuck a bit of roving onto the top to round out the point and needle felt it in place. Add more roving and felt as necessary to create an even and smooth point.

6 Cover the **BASE** of the cone by felting on a large tuft of green roving until smooth and level.

FIGURE 1

FIGURE 2

Created by Cathy Gaubert

SWEET
Sewing Room

The sewing room: a sacred spot for creative expression, artistic pursuits, and felt silliness. And, of course, a few critter friends to wreak havoc! Create details that mimic your own real space.

Little Miss Crafty

With a cute felt up-do, a fancy fabric skirt, and bendable arms, this little lady is ready for some serious crafting.

Finished Size
6 inches (15.2 cm) tall

Materials & Tools
Felting needles: 38 and 40 gauge
Foam felting mat
Chenille stems
Wool stuffing for core
Yellow-orange, red, white, black, flesh, and pink roving
Scissors
Small print fabric
Iron
Sewing needle and thread or sewing machine
6-inch (15.2 cm) piece of ⅛-inch (.3 cm) round elastic or similar

1 To create the **BODY** armature, bend a chenille stem in half to measure 5½ inches (14 cm).

2 Wrap tufts of wool stuffing around the top 3 inches (7.6 cm) of the armature to form the **HEAD** and **TORSO**, and carefully needle felt in place, taking care to avoid the chenille stem. Continue to add more wool until the form is approximately 2 inches (5.1 cm) around.

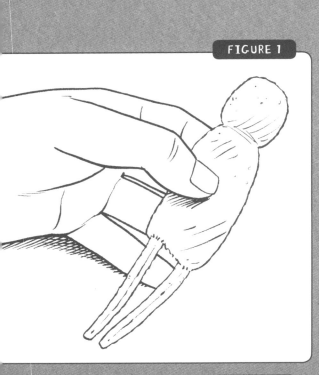

FIGURE 1

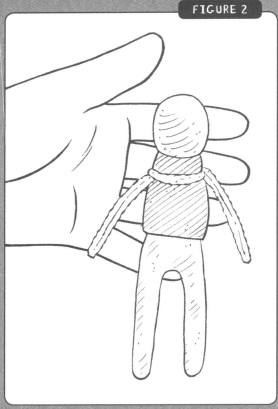

FIGURE 2

3 To create the head, lightly felt a neck about 1 inch (2.5 cm) down from the top of the form (fig. 1). Wrap tufts of flesh roving around the head and needle felt in place.

4 To create the BLOUSE, wrap tufts of red roving around the top of the body, beginning right below the neck. Needle felt in place (again taking care not to hit the chenille stem).

5 Working with one LEG at a time (bend the other one out of the way for now), wrap tufts of white roving around the leg and the bottom of the body. Needle felt carefully as there is not going to be much roving covering the chenille stem. Periodically roll the leg back and forth between your hands to smooth it out. Bend up the last ½ to ¾ inch (1.3 to 1.9 cm) of the leg to form her foot. Do the same for the other leg.

6 To form the ARMS, wrap a chenille stem around the torso, about ½ inch (1.3 cm) below the neck (fig. 2). Twist in back of the torso and bring the arms toward the front. Cut each arm to extend about 2 inches (5.1 cm) from the shoulder. Wrap the arms with tufts of red roving and needle felt in place, in the same manner as you did the legs. Take care while covering the chenille stem around the body as there will not be much wool covering it. Wrap flesh wool roving around the hands and needle felt in place.

I do love a good fabric sale!

7 To make her **HAIRDO**, hold her facing you, and attach tufts of the yellow-orange roving to the right side of the head first. Needle felt around the side and to the back of the head, too. Complete the left side in the same way. To make the little knotted side buns, take a tuft of yellow-orange roving about 4 inches (10.2 cm) long and ½ inch (1.3 cm) thick and twist from both ends, crisscrossing both ends to make a loose knot. Needle felt to the head through the middle of bun and felt random points where the bun dips and folds (fig. 3). Repeat for the other bun.

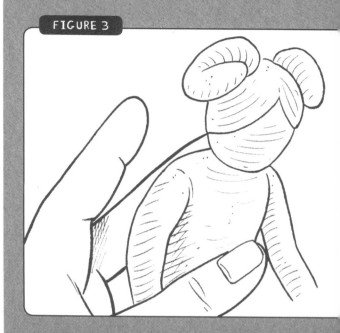

FIGURE 3

8 Roll two small tufts of black roving into small balls for the **EYES**. Gently felt onto the face. To give her a little gleam in the eye, add a tiny tuft of white roving to each eye and needle felt into place. With small tufts of pink roving, add a little blush to her **CHEEKS** by gently needle felting the pink wool below her eyes. For the **MOUTH**, roll a teeny tuft of red in between your fingers and needle felt into a slight smile.

9 For the **SKIRT**, choose a light fabric. Cut a piece 9 x 3½ inches (22.9 x 8.9 cm). Press up ⅛ inch (.3 cm) on the long side for the hem. Turn up again and press. Stitch the hem in place. Press up ⅛ inch (.3 cm) on the other long side and then fold up ½ inch (1.3 cm); press. This side will be the top of the skirt (we'll stitch the casing and add the elastic after we sew the skirt together).

10 With wrong sides together (and right sides facing out), stitch a ¼-inch (.6 cm) seam on the short side of the skirt. Turn right sides facing together (and wrong sides facing out), and press the seam. Stitch along the short side again to enclose the seam.

11 Fold the top of the skirt down on your previously pressed lines. Stitch about ¼ inch (.6 cm) from the top of the fold to make the casing, making sure to leave an opening where you can insert the elastic. Thread the elastic through the casing, knotting the ends together so that the skirt fits snuggly. Stitch the opening shut.

Sewing Machine

Create your sewing machine in miniature, complete with "working" needle and thread.

Finished Size
1¼ x 2 inches (3.2 x 5.1 cm)

Materials & Tools
Felting needles: 38 and 40 gauge
Foam felting mat
Red, white, and black roving
Flat-head pin
Bamboo skewer
Red thread
Glue (optional)

FIGURE 1

1 With white roving, make a rectangular shape approximately ¾ inch (1.9 cm) wide, ¾ inch (1.9 cm) deep, and 1¼ inches (3.2 cm) tall; this will be the part of the machine with the buttons. Next make another rectangular shape approximately ½ inch (1.3 cm) tall, ½ inch (1.3 cm) deep, and 1 inch (2.5 cm) long to form the arm. Needle felt the two pieces together. Wrap a tuft of white roving around the joint and needle felt until secure and smooth. Make a ½-inch (1.3 cm) cube and needle felt to the machine in the same manner to form the housing for the needle (fig. 1).

2 With a small tuft of black roving, needle felt one large KNOB. With teeny tufts of red and black roving, needle felt two smaller knobs above the larger one.

3 Push a flat-head pin through the top of the machine and out of the bottom, right where the NEEDLE would actually be. The tip of the pin should be flush with the base of the machine so that it can stand on its own; this will mean that the top of the pin sticks up out of the top of the machine a bit ... perfect for "threading" your needle.

4 Snip off a teeny bit of the bamboo skewer and wrap red thread around it to create a SPOOL OF THREAD for your machine. You may want to felt a small indention on the top of the machine (above the knobs) so that the spool can sit there without falling over. Of course, you can always use a smidge of glue if you would like to attach it there permanently. "Thread" the machine.

Companion Cat

A creative space needs a little creative distraction, and this kitty is happy to oblige.

Finished Size
2 inches (5.1 cm) tall

Materials & Tools
Felting needles: 38 and 40 gauge
Foam felting mat
Red, black, and natural gray roving
Pink and white thread
Sewing needle

1 With a tuft of natural gray roving, form a ball and needle felt to approximately ¾ inch (1.9 cm) in diameter for the **HEAD**. With a slightly larger tuft of natural gray roving, needle felt a thimble-shape for the **BODY**, approximately 1 inch (2.5 cm) tall with a 1-inch (2.5 cm) diameter base. Stack the head and body and gently needle felt to join the two pieces. Roll a small tuft of red roving into a rope and wrap around the neck (fig. 1). Needle felt to secure.

2 To make the **EARS**, pull two small tufts of natural gray roving and form into rough triangles. Needle felt into more defined triangles, but leave the bottoms rough. Place the ear on top of the head with the rough end lying on the back of the head. Felt in place (fig. 2). Do the same with the other ear.

3 For the **TAIL**, roll a tuft of natural gray roving into a 2¼-inch-long (5.7 cm) rope and gently felt, taking care to felt in one end. Felt the rough end on the back of the cat near the base.

4 Roll two teeny tufts of black roving into small balls for the **EYES**. Gently needle felt onto each side of the head.

5 Using pink thread, stitch a tiny **NOSE** and **MOUTH** on the face. Stitch through and knot three strands of white thread on each side of the face to create **WHISKERS**.

FIGURE 1

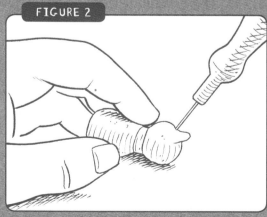

FIGURE 2

Little Bluebird

Who can create without a soundtrack?
A felt bluebird provides sweet tunes
for our crafty lady and for you.

Finished Size
1 x ½ inch (2.5 x 1.3 cm)

Materials & Tools
Felting needles: 38 and 40 gauge
Foam felting mat
Turquoise, orange, and black roving

FIGURE 1

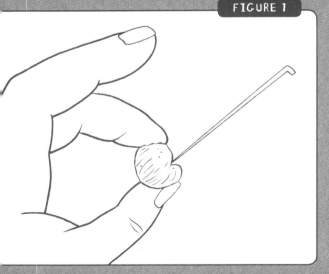

1 With a tuft of turquoise roving, begin felting a small ball, but leave a ½ to ¾-inch (1.3 to 1.9 cm) tail of roving to hold onto. After tightly felting that portion into a ½-inch (1.3 cm) ball, begin to felt the **TAIL** into shape (fig. 1).

2 Felt a tiny depression in the bird's face for the **BEAK**. Roll a teeny bit of orange roving and gently felt into a beak shape. Place the beak into the depression and carefully needle felt into place.

3 Roll two teeny tufts of black roving into small balls for the **EYES**. Gently needle felt onto each side of the head.

Finished Size
½ inch (1.3 cm) in diameter

Materials & Tools
Felting needles: 38 and 40 gauge
Foam felting mat
Red roving
Small pins with heads

Pincushion
Treasured tool of sewers and quilters, make sure your sewing room scene has at least one handy pincushion.

1 With a tuft of red roving, form a ball and needle felt to approximately ½ inch (1.3 cm) in diameter.

2 Snip the tips off of several small pins and stick them into the pincushion.

Finished Size
½ inch (1.3 cm) in diameter

Materials & Tools
Felting needles: 38 and 40 gauge
Foam felting mat
Wool roving in various colors
2 flat-head pins

Balls of Yarn
Art should just go ahead and imitate life: add some (felted) yarn stash to your craft space!

1 With tufts of roving in assorted colors, needle felt varying sizes of balls.

2 Poke two flat-head pins into one of the balls for knitting needles.

Land of the
DINOSAURS

Lost lands and extinct creatures live again! Recreate your favorite prehistoric flora and fauna in felt splendor, but do be mindful of the volcano.

T-Rex

The Tyrannosaurus Rex: majestic beast, deadly predator, humorously tiny arms.

Finished Size
10½ inches (26.7 cm) tall

Materials & Tools
Template (page 126)
Felting needle: 38 gauge
Foam felting mat
Core wool stuffing*
Light, medium, and dark shades of green wool roving
Small tufts of black and yellow wool roving
White craft felt
Scissors
Waxed thread
Sewing needle
*You'll need 1½ to 2 ounces (43 to 57 grams).

FIGURE 1

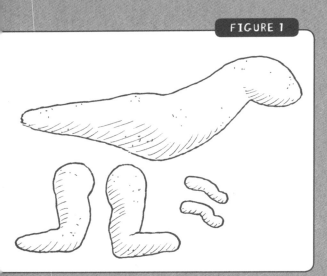

1 Loosely shape the T-Rex's **BODY** out of core wool stuffing: an oval shape like a squashed softball for the main body, a cone about 8 inches (20.3 cm) long for the tail, and a cylinder about 6 inches (15.2 cm) long for the neck. Keep one side of the cylinder and the fat end of the cone fluffy to allow plenty of loose wool to attach the pieces to the body. Securely felt the three pieces together in a straight line (fig. 1). Add extra core wool to the body to fill in the joining areas, to build up the rump for muscular legs, and to round out the head so that it's about the size and shape of an egg.

2 Separately needle felt the **ARMS** and **LEGS** out of core wool stuffing (fig. 1). These should be more tightly felted than the body pieces to help support the T-Rex when he stands. For the legs, you'll need two flattened egg shapes and two wide rectangles. Securely felt the egg shapes to the tops of the foot rectangles by poking down from the leg to the foot and up from the foot to the leg. For the arms, felt two very tiny tubes out of the core wool.

FIGURE 2

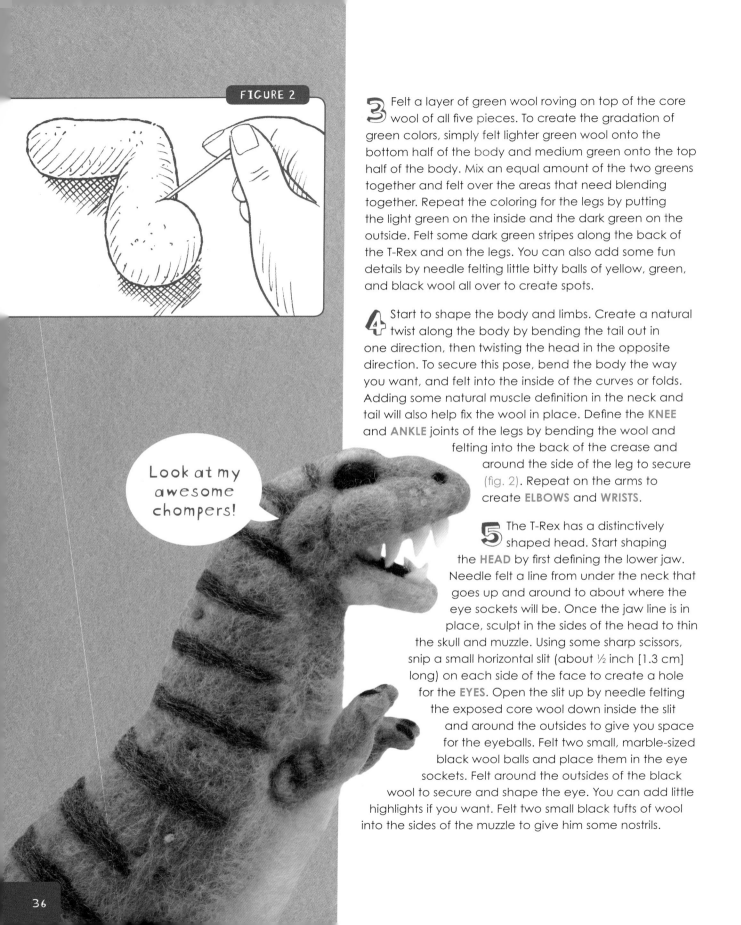

Look at my awesome chompers!

3 Felt a layer of green wool roving on top of the core wool of all five pieces. To create the gradation of green colors, simply felt lighter green wool onto the bottom half of the body and medium green onto the top half of the body. Mix an equal amount of the two greens together and felt over the areas that need blending together. Repeat the coloring for the legs by putting the light green on the inside and the dark green on the outside. Felt some dark green stripes along the back of the T-Rex and on the legs. You can also add some fun details by needle felting little bitty balls of yellow, green, and black wool all over to create spots.

4 Start to shape the body and limbs. Create a natural twist along the body by bending the tail out in one direction, then twisting the head in the opposite direction. To secure this pose, bend the body the way you want, and felt into the inside of the curves or folds. Adding some natural muscle definition in the neck and tail will also help fix the wool in place. Define the **KNEE** and **ANKLE** joints of the legs by bending the wool and felting into the back of the crease and around the side of the leg to secure (fig. 2). Repeat on the arms to create **ELBOWS** and **WRISTS**.

5 The T-Rex has a distinctively shaped head. Start shaping the **HEAD** by first defining the lower jaw. Needle felt a line from under the neck that goes up and around to about where the eye sockets will be. Once the jaw line is in place, sculpt in the sides of the head to thin the skull and muzzle. Using some sharp scissors, snip a small horizontal slit (about ½ inch [1.3 cm] long) on each side of the face to create a hole for the **EYES**. Open the slit up by needle felting the exposed core wool down inside the slit and around the outsides to give you space for the eyeballs. Felt two small, marble-sized black wool balls and place them in the eye sockets. Felt around the outsides of the black wool to secure and shape the eye. You can add little highlights if you want. Felt two small black tufts of wool into the sides of the muzzle to give him some nostrils.

6 Use your sharp scissors to cut the head open to create the giant growling **MOUTH**. Cut all the way through the wool roving and core wool. Felt the exposed core wool stuffing back, and cover it with a layer of black wool roving. Finish shaping the head by creating some chubby cheeks with a line from the corner of the mouth up and around to the outside corner of the eyes, and define the lower jowl with a felted line that goes from the corner of the mouth down and around the under side of the neck.

7 Trace and cut out the **TEETH** template from white craft felt. Line up the center of the teeth pattern with the center of the upper jaw. Needle felt the white felt into the mouth from both the front and back to secure (fig. 3). You'll have extra teeth hanging out of the sides, so trim the excess off and use one of the pieces for the bottom teeth. Center the trimmed-off teeth piece onto the center of the bottom jaw, and attach securely.

8 Finish the arms and legs by cutting and sculpting the claws. On each leg, cut the foot, about half way in, into three equal parts. Felt the three sections down to pointy toes with boney knuckles (fig. 4). Cover any exposed core wool with the matching green color, and felt some dark green wool onto the bottom of the foot. Cut the end of each arm into two (useless) pointy fingers (fig. 5), and cover any exposed core wool with green wool. Felt tiny tufts of black wool roving to create triangular claws on each toe and finger.

9 Time to attach the arms and legs! Thread thick or waxed string onto a large sewing needle. Start by sewing through one leg from the inside to the outside, leaving about 4 inches (10.2 cm) of extra string loose at the end. Make the first half of an "X" on the outside of the leg, then sew the string all the way through the leg, body, and out the other side of the opposite leg. Pull the string tight and cross to make half of an "X" on the second leg, sew all the way through all three parts back to the outside of the first leg. Pull tight, cross to finish the "X," sew through the body, and finish the "X" on the other leg. Sew through the leg and body, exiting on the inside of the first leg where the beginning loose string end is. Pull the string tight, tie a knot, and trim the extra off. Repeat to attach arms.

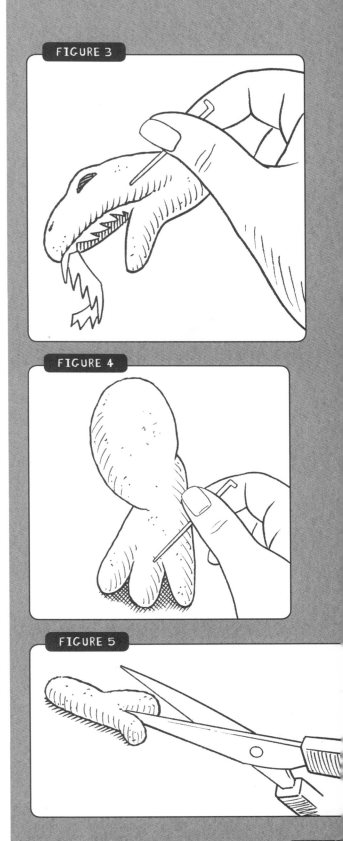

FIGURE 3

FIGURE 4

FIGURE 5

Stegosaurus

Needle felt your favorite Jurassic herbivore, with craft felt plates that are fashionable and functional!

Finished Size
12 x 7½ inches (30.5 x 19 cm)

Materials & Tools
Template (page 126)
Felting needle: 38 gauge
Foam felting mat
Core wool stuffing*
Light green and medium shades
   of green wool roving
Orange, yellow, and black roving
White craft felt
Scissors
*You'll need 1½ to 2 ounces
   (43 to 57 grams).

Yum... fan palms and ranch dressing!

1 Loosely felt core wool stuffing into the three shapes that'll make up the Stegosaurus's **BODY**: a large oval shape about the size of a squished softball, a cone shape about 8 inches (20.3 cm) long, and a tube shape around 6 inches (15.2 cm) long (fig. 1). Keep the wool on the fat end of the cone and one side of the tube fluffy to have extra wool to felt them to each other.

2 Felt the body shapes together, basically in a straight line. Securely felt the fluffy wool into the larger oval shape. Add extra core wool to fill in any lumpiness in the transition areas of the three pieces. Also add to fill out the roundness of the head and muzzle until it's about the size of a golf ball.

3 Needle felt a layer of the light green wool roving over the entire body. Add some variation to the green by needle felting very thin layers of darker green wool roving on top of the back. Gently pull small tufts of darker green roving apart till it's almost as thin as cobwebs. Felt thin layer after thin layer on to create the blended areas.

FIGURE 1

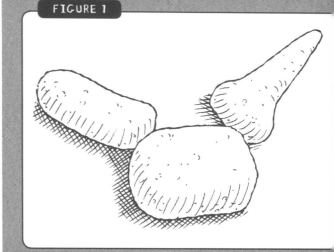

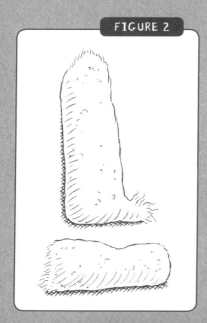

FIGURE 2

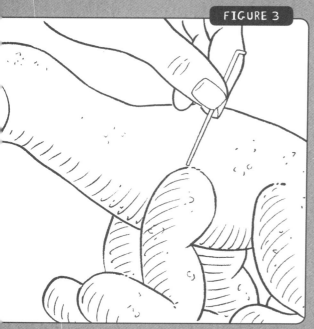

FIGURE 3

4 Start to shape the body of the Stegosaurus. Concentrate on twisting the body from the head to the tail by bending the wool and needle felting on the inside of the curves to secure the shape. For example, twist the tip of the tail up and away from the body and felt the inside until it stays in place. Twist and felt the neck in the opposite direction. Creating muscle definition along the neck and tail will also help secure the twisting pose.

5 Felt four tubes (about 4 inches [10.2 cm] long) and four squares (about 2 inches [5.1 cm]) out of the core wool stuffing to create the **LEGS** and **FEET** (fig. 2). Keep one end of the tubes fluffy to help felt to the squares. Securely felt the loose wool on the end of the tubes onto the top of the squares. Cover each leg with a layer of the lighter green wool roving, and add some darker green shading to the outside.

6 Define the shape of the legs by creating some folds that'll become the **KNEE** and **ANKLE** joints. Bend the tube a little so the felt creases, and felt the leg from the back and sides to secure the bend. Do the same for the ankle by squeezing the square foot shape, and the tube leg together and needle felting it from the front and sides. Add tiny wisps of darker green wool onto the feet to create lines for **TOES**. Repeat for all legs till you have four nice, chubby legs.

7 Attach the four legs to the Stegosaurus body. Start by placing the leg and felting the wool from the leg into the body. Felt the leg into the body until you can't imagine felting anymore (fig. 3). Then, felt the wool from the body into the leg; the more securely they are felted together, the more stable the Stegosaurus will be when it stands. Keep changing directions (leg to body, body to leg). You know you're done when you give the leg a good tug and it doesn't pull out.

8 Continue to shape and pose the body. Force the dinosaur into a pose you like, and then felt on the insides of any curves or folds to secure the shape. Think about the position of the legs and how the head hangs; these will all help define the character and action of the animal.

FIGURE 4

9 Trace the **FIN** templates onto the white craft felt. Cut out as many fins as will fit along the back of the Stegosaurus. Place them with the largest fin in the middle and taper down until there are several small ones at the tip of the tail and behind the head.

10 Felt a layer of orange and yellow wool roving onto both sides of the white wool fins. Felt the orange on the bottom of the fin (keeping the bottom fluffy), yellow on the top, and a mixture of both colors in the middle to help blend them together. Felt the fluffy orange wool from the bottom of the fins straight down into the body to securely attach them (fig. 4).

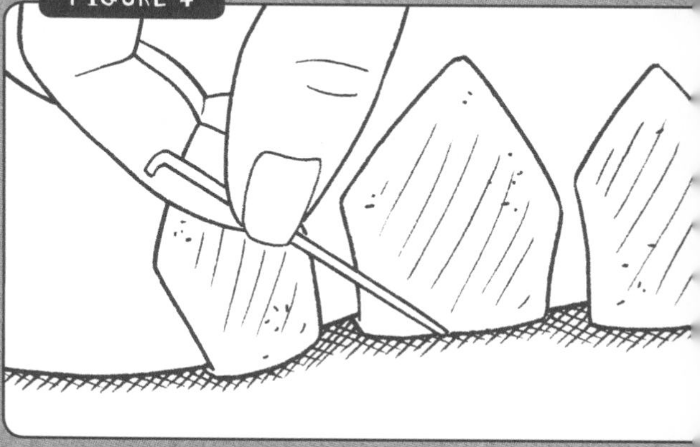

11 To shape the **HEAD**, felt the front of the face down to a tapered, blunt point (think of it like a beak). Felt a layer of darker green wool roving around the beak. Further define the **MOUTH** by felting the roving into a sharp line about half way back onto the head. Using a sharp pair of scissors, cut the beak open about one-third from the bottom and back to the defined dark green line. Felt the exposed core wool back into the mouth area, and cover with a layer of black wool roving. Felt some tiny black tufts onto the beak to create **NOSTRILS**.

12 Using sharp scissors, cut ¾-inch-long (1.9 cm) slits where the **EYES** will go. Open the eye socket up a little, place a small marble-sized black wool ball into the hole, and felt it into place; repeat for the second eye. Add a little sparkle to the Stegosaurus's eyes by felting some tiny orange highlights onto the eyeballs. Finish shaping the head by needle felting in a jaw line. Starting at the corner of the mouth, felt up and around the head into the corner of the eye socket to create some chubby cheeks.

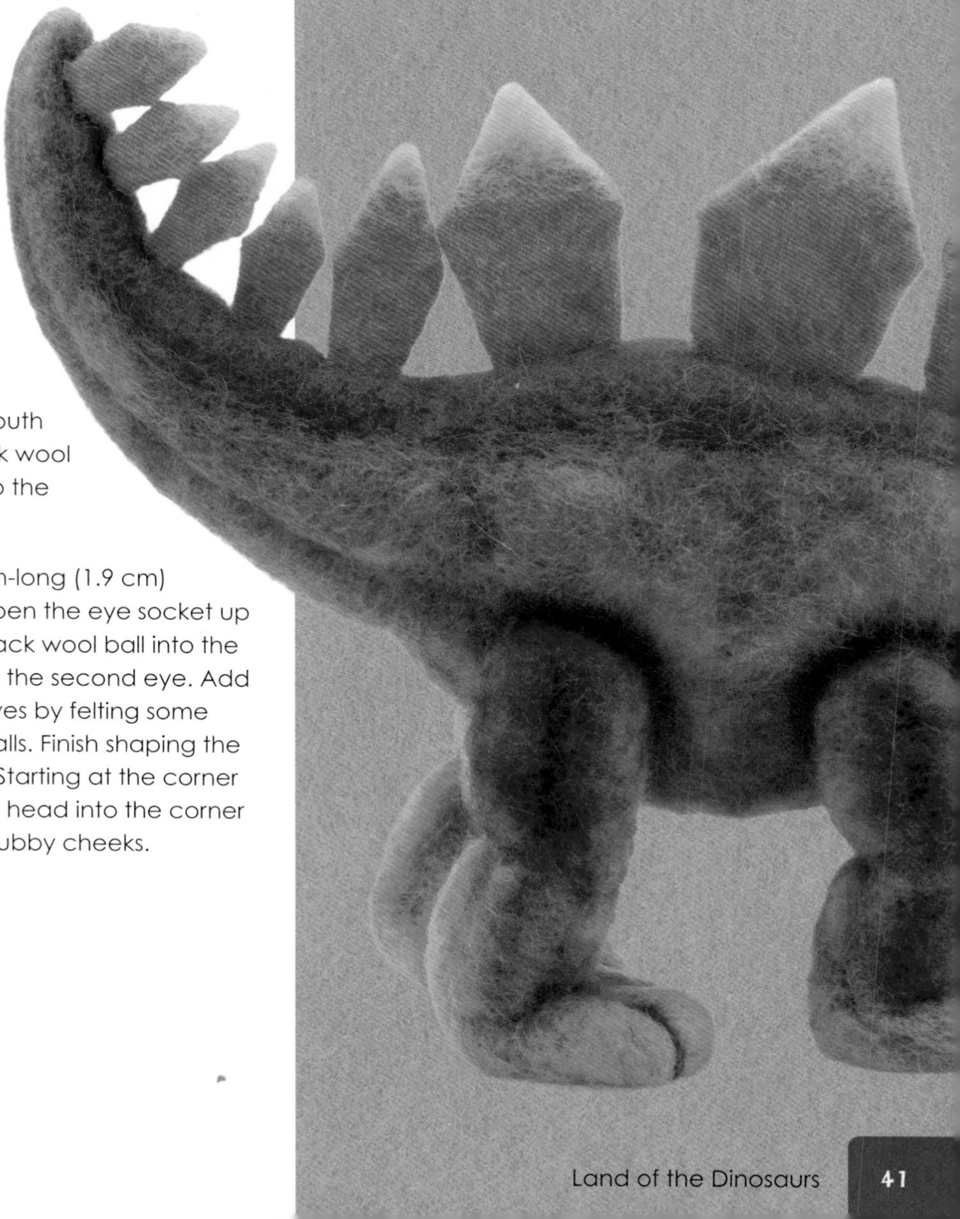

Giant Fern

Giant-sized like the creatures that roam among them, this fern's luscious leaves are created with craft felt and wire.

Finished Size
10 inches (25.4 cm) tall

Materials & Tools
Templates (page 126)
Felting needle: 38 gauge
Foam felting mat
Light green, dark green, light pink,
   and dark pink craft felt
Core wool stuffing
Tan, dark tan, and brown roving
Scissors
Wire cutters
22-gauge wire (or thin craft wire)
⅛-inch (.3 cm) wire (or other thick wire)
Glue gun
Needle-nose pliers

1 Trace and cut the **LEAF** and **STEM BASE** template shapes from both dark green and light green craft felt. You will need many leaves to create the feathery branches that are characteristic of a fern.

2 Snip the thin 22-gauge wire into four stem pieces: two longer wires, around 10 inches (25.4 cm), and two shorter wires, about 6 inches (15.2 cm).

3 Lay one end of a stem wire onto the middle of a felt leaf shape. Place a dot of hot glue on the wire and fold the leaf in half over the wire. Hold the leaf until the glue is set. Continue to glue additional leaves down the length of the wire, overlapping each new leaf about one-third over the previous one (fig. 1). Work until you've got about 3 inches (7.6 cm) of wire left uncovered. Apply hot glue half way down the uncovered wire, and wrap the stem base section of felt around it, keeping the bottom inch (2.5 cm) unglued so you'll have access to the wire. Repeat for the other three stem wires.

4 Trace and cut out four **FLOWER** template shapes from both the light and dark pink felt. Also, trace and cut out four flower template shapes from the light green felt.

5 Cut the ⅛-inch (.3 cm) wire to about 20 inches (50.8 cm) long. Place one end of the wire one-third of the way up on a light pink flower petal, apply hot glue on the wire, and fold the petal in half along the wire. Hold the petal in place until the glue is set. With a sharp pair of scissors, trim the square ends of the felt off, close to the wire along the glued seam. Flip the wire and petal over so that the seam is facing the opposite direction. Place the next flower petal about half way down the first, hot glue the wire, fold the petal in half, and hold (fig. 2). Trim the square ends of the felt along the glue seam and continue to glue the other light pink petals on, followed by the four dark pink petals.

6 Flip the wire over again so that most of the petal seams are facing down. Glue a green petal about half way down the last pink petal, and fold it in half, hold, and trim the edge. This will help make the green petals of the flower stem bend in the opposite direction from the flower petals. Repeat for the last three green petals.

7 At the bottom of the glued green flower petals, bend the thick wire at a 90° angle. Grab that point with the needle-nose pliers and bend the wire around the pliers in a flat spiral shape to create a sturdy base for the fern (fig. 3).

8 Felt some core wool stuffing into a dome-shaped **TRUNK** around the spiral base of the fern. Felt lightly, so you don't break the needle. Felt some additional core wool to the underside of the base to cover the wire. Place a flattened tuft of wool over the wire and poke it through the gaps in the wire. It will tighten itself up as you felt.

9 Insert one leaf stem wire into the wool trunk alongside the flower stem, but keep the green felt hanging on the outside of the wool (you may need to widen the hole with a little cut). Hot glue the stem wires together just above the trunk. Keep gluing the other leaf stems while arranging them like a flower bouquet, bending the stems and opening up the leaves.

10 Needle felt light tan wool roving over the fern's dome trunk. Use the unattached green felt to create tapered triangles that transition from the stems to the trunk. Felt deeper cracks into the trunk coming from the ends of the green stems. Add some darker tan wool for shading and darker brown wool roving into the cracks.

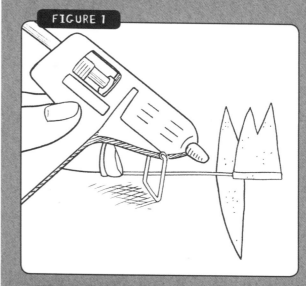

FIGURE 1

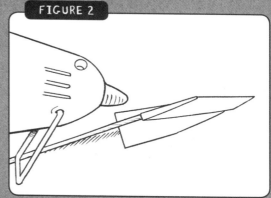

FIGURE 2

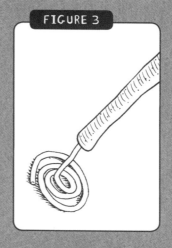

FIGURE 3

Spotty Dinosaur Eggs

Easily transform old bouncy balls into fun and fuzzy new toys ... who knows what'll hatch up!

Finished Size
1½ inches (3.8 cm) in diameter

Materials & Tools
Felting needle: 38 gauge
Foam felting mat
White roving
Small tufts of red, black, yellow, and orange roving
Bouncy balls or plastic eggs

1 Lay out several tufts of white wool roving so that they're about 1 inch (2.5 cm) wide by 4 inches (10.2 cm) long with a thin, even thickness. Wrap one tuft around the bouncy ball (or roll the ball up in the wool). Do this several times, each time wrapping in a different direction until the ball is evenly and completely covered.

2 Felt the wool around the ball until it's tight. Be sure to felt at an extreme angle, almost sideways, and not directly up and down. The needle will break easily if you poke the ball too many times.

3 Roll up tiny balls of colored wool roving between your fingers to felt on as spots. Layer different colors of spots on top of each other and use little wisps of roving as thin lines.

NOTE: *If you're using the bouncy balls for the dinosaur eggs, they will still bounce after you felt them. If plastic Easter eggs are in season, try putting a penny or small button inside the egg before felting so it will rattle!*

Fan Palms

The perfect hiding place for lesser beasts, these little fan palms are a snap to make with craft felt and glue, which stiffens the fronds.

Finished Size
5 x 2½ inches (12.7 x 6.4 cm)

Materials & Tools
Templates (page 126)
Scissors
Yellow, orange, and red craft felt
Glue gun
White craft glue
Aluminum foil

1 Trace and cut out nine palm **FROND** template shapes from the craft felt.

2 Line five palm fronds up together in a half circle shape divided at regular angles, like the spokes of a wheel. Place a dot of hot glue on the flat bottom edge of the first palm frond. Press the second frond firmly onto the glue at a 45° angle. Glue the third frond on top of the second at a 45° angle, followed by the fourth frond at a 45° angle, and finally the fifth frond on a flat line with the first. It's important that the palm frond has a flat bottom so that it'll sit upright after it's stiffened with the craft glue.

3 Glue the four remaining fronds onto the back of the fan with little dots of hot glue, dividing the spaces evenly between the front fronds. Trim any overhanging felt corners or spots of dried glue that might be sticking out at weird angles.

4 Water down some white craft glue in a bowl until it's a little thicker than milk. Dip the whole fan palm into the glue, and completely soak it. Squeeze out most of the extra glue.

5 Crumple up some aluminum foil so that it's a flattened puck shape. Drape the fan palm face up over the aluminum foil (fig. 1). Double-check that the bottom fronds are still in a straight line. Let the felt completely dry; it might take a day or two but it will be sturdy and stiff once it's dry.

FIGURE 1

Dinosaur Fossils

This felt fossil is strung together in one piece, so you can position it many different ways.

Finished Size
8 x 3 inches (20.3 x 7.6 cm)

Materials & Tools
Felting needle: 38 gauge
Foam felting mat
White wool roving
Small tuft of black roving
Scissors
White sewing thread
Sewing needle

1 Pull out a tuft of white wool roving that is about 1 inch (2.5 cm) wide by 6 inches (15.2 cm) long. Lightly stretch the wool until it has an even thickness, and begin to roll it between your palms. Keep rolling it to compress and felt it. Make about four rolls that are 6 inches (15.2 cm) long by ½ inch (1.3 cm) in diameter.

2 Cut the ropes with a sharp pair of scissors to create all the bones for the skeleton. You will need several sizes of bones: about fifteen ½-inch (1.3 cm) pieces for the backbones and toes, and seven 2-inch (5.1 cm) pieces for the ribs and legs. Once all the pieces of rope are cut, simply rub them between your palms to tighten the ends up.

3 Take three of the 2-inch (5.1 cm) pieces and snip the ends to a point. Felt these three pointy pieces to the center of three ½-inch (1.3 cm) pieces to make **RIBS**. You can make the ribs curve by slightly bending the rib and needle felting on the inside of the curve.

4 Felt two small tufts of fluffy white wool into bean shapes, working directly on your foam surface. Felt these two beans onto the ends of two 2-inch (5.1 cm) leg bone pieces. Now you have a **HIP BONE** and **SHOULDER BLADE!**

5 To make the **TOES**, start by trimming the ends of six ½-inch (1.3 cm) pieces to pointy ends. Lay three pieces out in an arrow shape and felt the flat ends together.

6 To make the **HEAD**, create an egg shape (a little smaller than a golf ball) out of the white wool roving. Shape down one side so that it becomes a flat, rounded snout. Felt in two larger holes for eye sockets and two smaller ones for the nose. Felt little tufts of black wool into them. Mix a tiny bit of black and white wool roving together and felt it on for some shading.

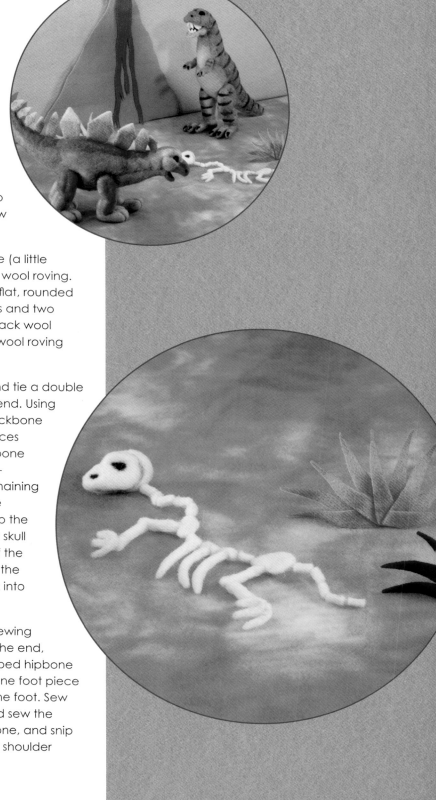

7 Pull out a long piece of white thread, and tie a double knot about 4 inches (10.2 cm) from the end. Using a thin sewing needle, start to thread the backbone pieces on. Thread half of the backbone pieces on, thread on one of the bean-shaped hipbone pieces, the three rib pieces, the other bean-shaped shoulder piece, followed by the remaining backbone pieces. Next, sew up through the middle of the skull. Knot the thread closely to the front of the skull, then sew back through the skull and snip the thread (this will hide the end of the thread). Thread the 4-inch (10.2 cm) end of the thread onto the sewing needle. Sew it back into the line of backbones to hide it.

8 Thread a new piece of string onto the sewing needle. Knot it 4 inches (10.2 cm) from the end, and sew it through the top of the bean-shaped hipbone and leg. Tightly thread one leg piece and one foot piece onto the string, and knot at the bottom of the foot. Sew the string back up into the foot and leg, and sew the loose end of the thread back into the hipbone, and snip the loose threads. Repeat for the remaining shoulder blade, leg, and foot pieces.

The Felt Galaxy ...
AND BEYOND!

Travel to a new felt world for some exploring, and catch a few tv shows with your new alien friends. Then you're off to find more felt worlds in your rocket ship!

Alien Girl

With pose-able tentacle arms, this sweet alien gal spends her free time studying Earth culture and loves watching her favorite Earth programs on television.

Finished Size
4½ inches (11.4 cm) tall

Materials & Tools
Felting needle: 40 gauge
Foam felting mat
Polyester fiberfill*
Light green, magenta, orange, white, pink, and black roving
Chenille stem
Sewing pins, size 24, in magenta (for antenna)
Craft glue (optional)
*You'll need ½ ounce (14 grams).

1. Create a **BODY** base out of polyester fiberfill. Fold and felt a portion of polyester fiberfill into a tapered, bell-like shape. Add fiber to the bottom to create a sturdy, flared bottom (fig. 1).

2. Fold and felt a smaller portion of polyester fiberfill to create a ball for the **HEAD**, approximately half as tall as the body base.

3. Felt light green wool onto the bottom third of the body base. Create dimension by needle felting more aggressively to create small recesses and adding additional fiber if necessary to create curves.

4. To create the alien's **SHIRT**, needle felt magenta wool into the remaining top two-thirds of the body base. To add dimension and simulate a soft, rounded, clothing-like feeling, needle felt a length of additional magenta wool around the bottom edge of this section and sculpt a rounded bump.

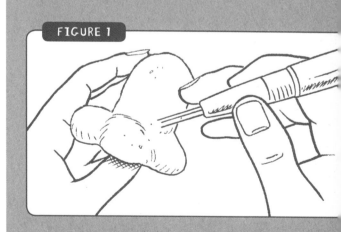
FIGURE 1

FIGURE 2

5 To make the **ARM**, cut a length of chenille stem approximately the length of the body's height. Designate one end of the chenille stem the **HAND**. Wrap a length of green wool around the chenille stem and felt slightly to secure (fig. 2), starting from the hand end and working down. Increase the thickness gradually as you continue to wrap away from the hand, wrapping wool around the chenille stem several times.

6 After wrapping, felt gently to bind the fibers together tightly. Felt carefully around the hand to create a rounded tip. Continue to add fiber and felt until the chenille stem is no longer visible. Repeat for the other arm.

7 Cover the round head base with light green wool until no white is visible, needle felting until smooth.

8 Portion out a length of orange wool and begin to loosely felt it into the green wool on the head to create **HAIR**. Leaving a square area uncovered on the front for the face, sculpt the hair into the desired style (fig. 3), adding extra wool if necessary to create volume. Fold the wool ends up and underneath the top layer to create a curved, finished edge and dimension. Felt to desired smoothness and firmness. Create definition lines carefully where the orange and green wools come together to frame the face. Create parts in the hair.

FIGURE 3

9 Portion out small pieces of black wool for **EYES**. Roll the small pieces between your fingers to create small oval balls of equal size. Using a single needle, felt the black wool until it adheres to the light green roving. Shape the eyes until they're smooth and slightly recessed into the body for depth.

I know: I'm adorable!

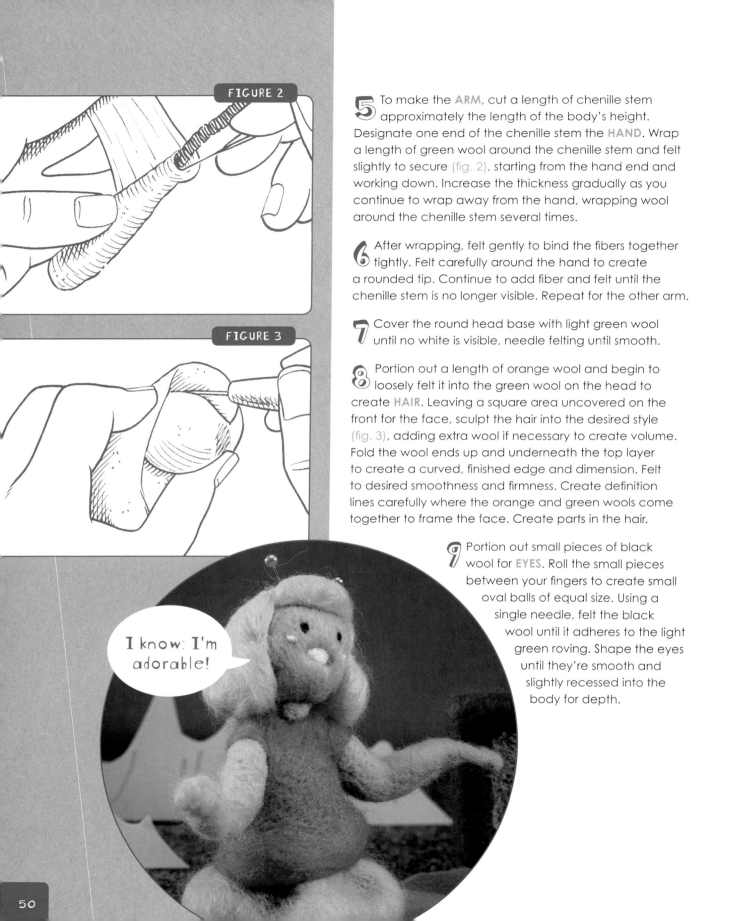

10 Felt white wool into a half circle shape to create the MOUTH. Felt the edges of the mouth to create definition and finish.

11 Portion out small pieces of pink wool for the CHEEK highlights. Roll the pieces between your fingers to create small oval balls of equal size. Felt the highlights in place on the face.

12 Place the head on top of the body shape. Needle felt around the bottom of the head until it attaches to the body. Strengthen the connection by needle felting up through the body into the head until it is securely attached.

13 Directly underneath the head, felt a small portion of light green roving into a half-circle shape on the magenta wool to form a NECK. Felt the green wool until it is slightly below the level of the magenta to create dimension.

14 Press the top of the arm to the body underneath the head. Felt a portion of magenta wool across the top of the arm, creating a shirtsleeve and attaching the arm at the shoulder (fig. 4). Continue needle felting until the arm is securely attached and then repeat for the other arm. The arms can now be posed into shape by carefully bending the chenille stem inside.

15 Create the alien ANTENNA by pushing the two sewing pins into the top of the head, approximately 1 inch (2.5 cm) apart. For extra stability, add a small dab of glue to the sharp end of the pin before carefully sticking it into the fiber!

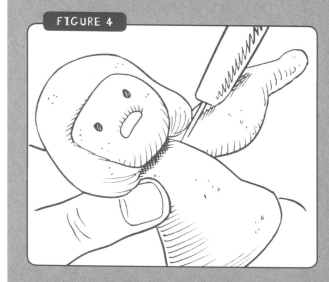

FIGURE 4

Big Purple Alien Blob

Huggable and utterly lovable, this friendly alien blob loves making friends, playing sports, shopping, and taking long walks along the lunar landscape.

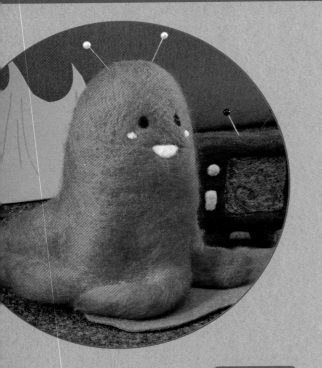

Finished Size
5 inches (12.7 cm) tall

Materials & Tools
Felting needle: 40 gauge
Foam felting mat
Polyester fiberfill*
Magenta**, pink, white, and black roving
Sewing pins, size 24, in white (for antenna)
Craft glue (optional)
*You'll need 2 ounces (57 grams).
**You'll need 1 ounce (28 grams) of this color.

1 Using polyester fiberfill, create a core shape for the BODY (fig. 1). Felt the fiber together into a rounded, tapered cone shape. Add additional polyester fiberfill to the bottom and back to extend the size and to create a base for the tentacles.

2 Sculpt five TENTACLES of varying size (fig. 2), curving and shaping as desired by needle felting additional polyester fiberfill to the main base to create dimension and length. Create recesses and curves by needle felting these areas more intensely. Keep needle felting the base until it is firm.

3 Cover the base with magenta wool, starting at the top and winding the wool down to the bottom. Felt magenta roving onto into the polyester fiberfill until it binds together, covering the base completely until no white is visible.

4 While covering the tentacles, continue shaping and adding definition by needle felting roving and adding magenta to create bulk and dimension as necessary.

FIGURE 1

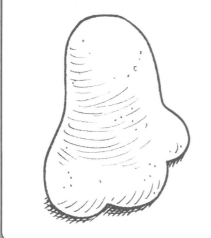

What's on the tellie today?

5. Choose one side of the figure to be the front. Portion out small pieces of black roving for the EYES. Roll the small pieces between your fingers to create small oval balls of equal size. Needle felt the black roving until it adheres to the magenta roving. Felt and shape the eyes until smooth and slightly recessed into the face to create dimension.

6. Using the photo as a guide, felt white roving into a half circle shape to create a smiling MOUTH. Felt the edges of the mouth to create definition and finish.

7. Portion out small pieces of pink roving for the CHEEK highlights. Roll the pieces between your fingers to create small oval balls of equal size. Needle felt the cheek highlights in place on the face.

8. Create the alien ANTENNA by pushing the two sewing pins into the top of the head, approximately 1 inch (2.5 cm) apart. For extra stability, add a small dab of glue to the sharp end of the pin before carefully sticking it into the fiber.

FIGURE 2

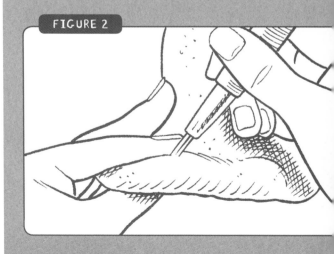

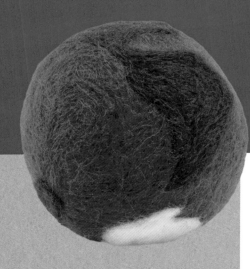

Blue Planet

Create your own felt solar system based on this simple planet, which may indeed support felted life forms.

Finished Size
3 inches (7.6 cm) in diameter

Materials & Tools
Felting needle: 40 gauge
Foam felting mat
Polyester fiberfill*
Blue, green, and white roving
*You'll need 1 ounce (28 grams).

FIGURE 1

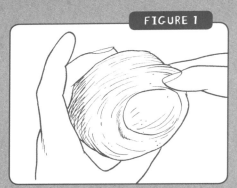

FIGURE 2

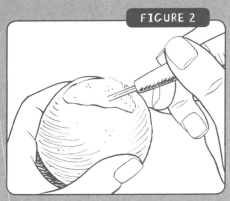

1 Using the polyester fiberfill, create a spherical CORE. Roll the polyester fiberfill into a ball and felt into the ball until it begins to bind together into an even, spherical shape. Add blue roving until the ball reaches the desired size. Continue rotating and needle felting the sphere until it is firm and the core is covered with blue roving (fig. 1).

2 Portion out several pieces of green roving. Felt each piece of the green roving into shapes on the blue base to create CONTINENTS. Continue to felt the roving until it binds together. If you like, felt the surface until it's smooth or leave the texture as is to create a more "land-like," organic feeling.

3 Portion out pieces of white roving. Felt the white wool into shapes on the top and bottom of the planet (fig. 2) to create icy North and South POLES.

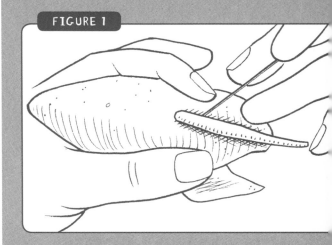

Rocket Ship

Ground control, we have lift off! In bright turquoise and red with three craft felt fins, this rocket's ready for its next mission.

1 To form the **SHIP**, create a polyester fiberfill core in the shape of a long cylinder. Taper the ends by pressing the fiber together firmly with your fingers and carefully needle felting around the area until it binds together into the desired shape. Shape one end into a rounded point to create the top, and create the bottom end by tapering to a flat circle. Add extra dimension to the middle of the core by needle felting additional fiber around the center.

2 Cover the core with turquoise wool and felt it down until the wool binds to the core and the surface is smooth and in the desired shape.

3 Create the bottom of the ship by wrapping a small piece of red wool around the bottom and needle felting it into the flat end.

4 Using a single needle, sculpt a line to differentiate the main body from the red tip.

5 Using the **FIN** template, cut six identical fin pieces from the red craft felt. Match the cut fins into pairs. Felt each pair of felt shapes together to form a thick sheet of wool.

6 Place three fins onto the ship body at equal intervals. The fins should extend beyond the bottom of the body by approximately ¼ inch (.6 cm). Place one fin on the body vertically, and felt along the fin's edges to attach it to the body (fig. 1). Repeat this step for all three fins.

7 Choose one side of the ship to be the front where the **WINDOW** will be positioned. Felt a small portion of white wool to the ship halfway between the top of the fins and the nose of the ship, making sure it is positioned in the middle of two fins. Continue to felt the white wool into the body, creating a circle.

FIGURE 1

Toy UFO

Unidentified flying object—identified! This saucer is the typical vehicle on this distant planet, zooming through the purple skies.

1 Roll a small piece of fiberfill together and needle felt it evenly to create a small spherical shape.

2 Portion the remaining polyester fiberfill into a long strip. Wind this fiber around the bottom of the small sphere to create a shallow SAUCER, needle felting it evenly. Press the fiber together and felt it together to create a thin rim.

3 Felt the underside of the saucer and add fiber until flat.

4 Felt a small piece of light blue wool around the top sphere.

5 Using gray wool, cover the bottom half of the base until no white is visible and the texture is smooth (fig. 1). Continue shaping the saucer until it slopes slightly downward by placing your thumb on the underside of the saucer and pressing down with a finger, felting carefully to bind the fibers together.

6 Portion out three pieces of gray wool to create the tripod LEGS. Roll one piece into a small triangle-like shape and needle felt until it binds tightly together. Repeat for the second and third pieces.

7 Attach each leg to the bottom of the saucer, felting into the shape until it binds securely to the saucer. Evenly space the legs so that the toy sits stably.

8 Portion out a small piece of black wool. Felt the roving into a very thin line where the light blue roving meets the gray roving to create definition between the saucer and window sections (fig. 2).

9 Create a small, triangular highlight in the window by felting a few strands of white wool onto the light blue sphere. Position the highlight so that it is slightly off-center.

FIGURE 1

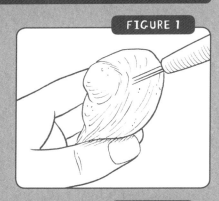

FIGURE 2

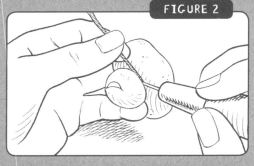

Old Timey Television

Despite spotty reception, this project can be personalized by felting a colorful scene onto the television screen.

Finished Size
2¾ inches (7 cm) square

Materials & Tools
Felting needle: 40 gauge
Foam felting mat
Polyester fiberfill*
Brown, gray, and white roving
Sewing pins, size 24, in black (for antenna)
*You'll need ½ ounce (14 grams).

1 Fold, press, and needle felt a portion of polyester fiberfill together to create a rectangular CORE. Continue wrapping fiber around this core until the desired size and shape is created. Define the rectangular edges by pressing the edges of the fiber core together and needle felting until a rounded corner is created. The shape does not need to be precisely rectangular or even.

2 Wrap the core in brown roving and felt the fiber until it adheres to the polyester fiberfill. Continue to add brown fiber until no white is showing.

3 To create a LEG, roll a piece of brown wool into a small barrel shape. Felt the shape until it adheres together, leaving a small tail of unfelted roving. Create two. Attach the legs at even intervals on the bottom edge of the main rectangle.

4 Felt a square of gray wool onto the rectangular base (fig. 1) to make the SCREEN, covering approximately the right three-fourths of the rectangle. Leave an outer edge of brown fiber visible to create the outer rim.

5 Felt the gray fiber square until it is slightly recessed to create a dimensional appearance.

6 Felt a small circle and rectangle of white fiber into the larger, left-hand rim to create a KNOB and KEYPAD detail (fig. 2). Add the antenna and extra details as desired.

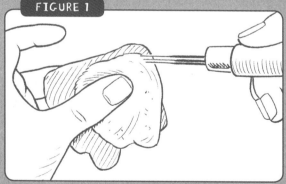

FIGURE 1

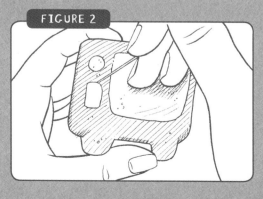

FIGURE 2

Circus MAXIMUS

This felt circus is maximum fun, with a ringmaster and two impressive attractions. Add additional sideshows and other characters to round out your cast.

Created by Heide Murray

Bird Ringmaster

This dapper fellow welcomes you with his fancy felt top hat and his adorable demeanor.

Finished Size

6 inches (15.2 cm) tall

Materials & Tools

Felting needles: 38 and 40 gauge
Foam felting mat
Red*, white, black, orange, and yellow roving
Dowel or bamboo skewer
4 black chenille stems, 12 inches (30.5 cm) long
1 black chenille stem, 4 inches (10.2 cm) long
  (for the baton)
Waxed polyester string, 18 inches (45.7 cm) long
Sewing needle with a large eye
Scissors
Wooden bead, less than ½ inch (1.3 cm)
  in diameter
Glue gun, fabric glue, and craft glue
Circular wooden disk
Glitter or sawdust
Awl
*You'll need ½ ounce (14 grams) of this color.

1 To make the HEAD, pull off 6-inch (15.2 cm) lengths of the red wool roving. If the roving is thick, split it in half lengthwise.

2 Make a slightly flattened ball for the bird's head. Using the pointed end of the dowel (moisten it a bit so the wool will stick), slowly and firmly spin the wool onto the dowel. Add each segment on top of the last, pulling firmly. When you almost have a 2-inch (5.1 cm) diameter through the thickest part, carefully pull the ball off the dowel. The head should be firm, but not squishy.

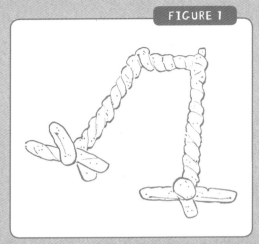

FIGURE 1

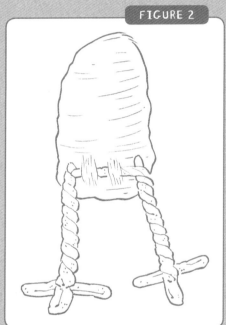

FIGURE 2

3 Loosely wrap several lengths of red wool perpendicularly over the swirled ends, and needle felt them, starting with the size 38 needle. After felting the ball all around, roll it around in your hands to smooth, and continue to felt. As you work, add small tufts of wool to make the surface even and firm. The finished size of the head should be about 2 inches (5.1 cm) in diameter in the thickest part.

4 Now it's time to make the **FACE**. Working with 1-inch (2.5 cm) tufts of white wool roving, begin shaping the face into a rough heart shape on the head, working from the outside into the middle. Use the needle to gently draw the outlines of the face as you felt it. Do not hold the wool down; let the tufts get imbedded into the head. Keep adding wool until no red color shows through the face.

5 Starting with a small triangle shape in the middle of the heart-shaped face, add and shape orange roving with the needle until the **BEAK** becomes three dimensional. For the **EYES**, split a very small amount of black wool into two equal tufts. Place the tuft of wool over the eye area and felt straight down into the face in a very small round design. Repeat for the other eye. Now roll the finished head gently in your hands, and then lightly needle felt the whole surface with the size 40 needle until it looks finished.

6 To make the **BODY**, bend and shape the legs and feet of the bird using the 12-inch (30.5 cm) chenille stems (fig. 1). Remember, his legs have to support his body weight.

7 Wrap an oblong ball of red roving on your dowel to start the body. It should be about 3 inches (7.6 cm) long and 1½ inches (3.8 cm) wide once it has been felted a few times. Attach the lightly felted body to the top of the legs by wrapping wool roving around the body and the legs (fig. 2). Crisscross the wool wraps (one vertical then one horizontal) and needle felt as you finish each wrap. Make sure the body is not moving on the legs by adding some wool around each leg and needle felting to the body. Needle felt carefully around the pipe cleaners as the wire can break the needle if hit too hard.

8 Pull two 5-inch (12.7 cm) segments of red wool from the roving for the **WINGS** and for the **TAIL**. Split one of them in two equal sections for the wings. Wind the two wings around the dowel and remove (fig. 3), place them on the foam, and needle felt one end and the sides until they are firm wing shapes. Be sure to leave fluff on one end of each to join them to the body (fig. 4). Fold the other wool segment into a triangle shape to create the tail. Needle felt it on the foam until firm, leaving one point fluffy and adding more wool if you need to. Needle felt the wings and tail onto the body. Add small tufts of red to blend. When the body is done, add the white chest, black bow tie, and black buttons with small tufts of wool.

9 To attach the head to the body, with your needle and polyester thread, sew up from under the tail and come out the neck area. Thread the needle through the wooden bead then through the head. Then sew it back down through the head, bead, and body ¼ inch (.6 cm) from where you started.

10 Make a square knot or two and pull them tight enough so the head is tight to the body. The bead may be hidden, but it will act as a joint. Sew the tails of the thread back into the body and cut them flush where you come out. You can tighten the head by pulling the thread tails back out and retying the knot if you need to.

11 Create the **TOP HAT** by winding a short length of black wool onto the dowel to make a cylinder. Remove the dowel, felt the top and bottom flat, and felt the sides until smooth. Then needle felt a black circle on the foam to be the brim, and needle felt the two pieces together. Add a red hatband with a very thin piece of red roving. With a small amount of glue, attach the hat to the head and felt the brim down into the head a bit.

12 Glue the ringmaster's feet to the wooden base, and then cover the base completely with craft glue and a layer of glitter or sawdust.

13 For the **BATON**, wind a bit of yellow wool roving around one end of the 4-inch (10.2 cm) length of black chenille, and felt into a ball shape. Using the awl, poke a hole through one wing, and position the baton in place. Fold up the bottom end of the chenille ¼ inch (.6 cm).

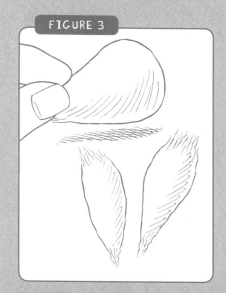

FIGURE 3

FIGURE 4

Welcome to our show!

Lion Strongman

The strong-yet-lovable lion will have you swooning on the midway with his felt muscles and his luscious pom-pom mane.

FIGURE 1

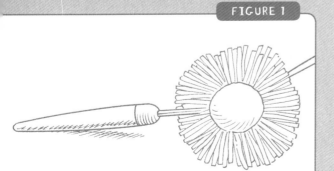

1 To create the MANE, begin by making a 3-inch (7.6 cm) diameter pom-pom with the yellow yarn. Make it thick, and tie it very tightly with waxed polyester thread, leaving long thread trails (as these will be sewn through the body to attach the head). Trim the pom-pom with sharp scissors until even.

2 Open up one side of the pom-pom, where you want the FACE to be, and needle felt in several tufts of yellow wool roving one on top of the other until you get a nice rounded dome (fig. 1).

Finished Size

6½ inches (16.5 cm) tall

Materials & Tools

Foam felting mat

Felting needles: 38 and 40 gauge

Pom-pom maker, for 3-inch (7.6 cm) diameter
   pom-pom

Yellow wool yarn

Yellow, black, and red roving

Waxed polyester string, 18 inches (45.7 cm) long

Scissors

Dowel or bamboo skewer

3 yellow chenille stems, 12 inches (30.5 cm) long

1 black chenille stem, 3 inches (7.6 cm) long

Sewing needle with a large eye

Wooden bead, less than ½ inch (1.3 cm)
   in diameter

Small two-hole button

Awl

White glue

Cardboard

Yellow thread

FIGURE 2

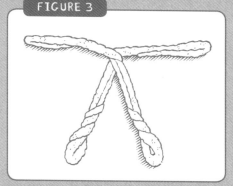

FIGURE 3

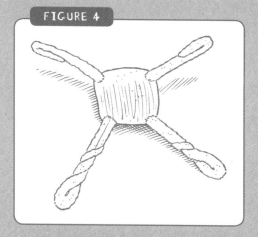

FIGURE 4

3 Making sure the thread tails of the pom-pom are pointing down, needle felt on the **NOSE**, **MOUTH**, and **EYES** (fig. 2). Use small tufts of black wool and make sure they sink down into the head. For each **EAR**, wind a small tuft of yellow roving on a dowel, remove it, and felt the tops and sides. Place the fluffy end of the ear into the mane and felt in place.

4 To create the **BODY**, start with two 12-inch (30.5 cm) yellow chenille stems wound together in the middle, with the **ARMS** and **LEGS** folded back on themselves (fig. 3). Add another yellow chenille stem to support the legs so your lion will be strong enough to stand. Wind several lengths of yellow wool roving around each leg and arm, and then around the middle to make the torso (fig. 4). Felt carefully as the wire in the chenille stems can break the needle easily.

5 Wind yellow wool up and down the arms and legs and needle felt very carefully. Wind a bit more fiber over the hands and feet to make them thicker. Blend all joints smoothly into the body with tufts of wool. Add any details like cute black shorts and a red belt before adding the head to the body.

6 Thread the waxed polyester thread attached to the head through the sewing needle, and sew down through the round wood bead, through the body, and out through the tail area (the thread will become his tail). Do the same with the other thread. Pull one thread through each hole in the small button, and tie knots. The button keeps the thread from sinking into the body and making the head loose. After tying a few square knots in the threads, wind a small amount of yellow roving around the thread ends and needle felt over them to create a TAIL. Then tie a little puff of yellow roving on the end of the tail and cut off the excess threads.

7 To create the DUMBELLS, needle felt two black balls of equal size and add numbers on both with white wool. Use an awl to make holes all the way though both balls. Put a dab of white glue on the ends of the 3-inch (7.6 cm) black chenille stem and put a ball on each end. Bend the lion's hand around the dumbbell so he looks super strong.

8 To create the RISER (for the lion and the elephant), cut out a 3-inch (7.6 cm) cardboard circle, and punch a small hole in the middle. Put this circle on your dowel and wind yellow roving tightly around the dowel, using the circle to keep the bottom flat. Add wool until the riser measures about 2 inches (5.1 cm) in diameter and very carefully take off the cardboard circle and the wool riser.

9 Needle felt the top, bottom, and the sides very well. Add the red details and a star on top.

TIP: *The risers can be made in varying sizes for the different performers.*

10 Stand the lion on the riser, and sew his feet down very tightly with thread that matches his feet.

Materials & Tools

Finished Size
5½ inches (14 cm) tall

Materials & Tools
Felting needles: 38 and 40 gauge
Foam felting mat
Gray*, yellow, black, red, and orange
  wool roving
Dowel or bamboo skewer
Wooden bead, less than ½ inch (1.3 cm)
  in diameter
3 black chenille stems, 12 inches (30.5 cm) long
1 black chenille stem, 3 inches (7.6 cm) long
Cardboard
Waxed polyester string, 18 inches (45.7 cm) long
Sewing needle with a large eye
Small button
Scissors
Black floss
You'll need ½ ounce (14 grams) of this color.

Fire-Breathing Elephant

Beware of the cuteness of this talented elephant! Able to breath fire and water, and a snazzy dresser to boot.

1 To create the **HEAD**, pull off 6-inch (15.2 cm) lengths of the gray wool roving. If the roving is thick, split it in half lengthwise.

2 Make a slightly flattened ball for the elephant's head. Using the pointed end of the dowel, spin the gray wool onto the dowel. Add each segment on top of the last, pulling firmly. When the ball is 2-inch (5.1 cm) diameter through the thickest part, carefully pull the ball off the dowel.

3 Loosely wrap several lengths of wool perpendicularly over the swirled ends, and needle felt them, working with the size 38 needle. After felting the ball all around, roll it around in your hands to smooth, and continue to felt. As you work, add small tufts of wool to make the surface even and firm. The finished size of the head should be about 2 inches (5.1 cm) in diameter in the thickest part.

4 Make two **EARS** by folding two 6-inch (15.2 cm) sections of gray roving on itself and needle felting the sections into ovals. Flip them over several times and work all the edges except where they will attach to the head; leave those fluffy. Attach the ears and blend into the head with small tufts of gray wool.

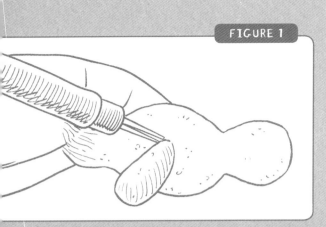

FIGURE 1

5 Wind a TRUNK shape on the dowel. Needle felt the sides and one end until firm. Attach the trunk to the lower middle of the face and blend (fig. 1). Add the EYES and EYEBROWS with black wool. Create a diamond shape on the top of the head with yellow wool and a red accent for the headpiece.

6 Start the BODY with two 12-inch (30.5 cm) black chenille stems wound together in the middle with the ARMS and LEGS folded back onto themselves (as you did for the lion in step 4). Add another black chenille stem to the legs so your elephant will be strong enough to hold his own weight. Wind several lengths of gray wool roving around the legs, arms, and around the middle to make the torso.

7 Wind gray wool up and down the arms and legs and needle felt very carefully on your foam. Wind a bit more fiber over the hands and feet to make them thicker. Blend all the joints smoothly into the body with tufts of wool. Add any details like cute yellow shorts and red shoes before sewing the head on to the body.

8 With your needle and polyester thread, sew up from the tail area and come out the neck area. Sew the needle as follows: through the wooden bead, through the head, out behind one ear, back in and across to the back of the other ear, and then down and out the neck area, through the bead and back through the body, coming out next to your starting place. Pull the threads through the buttonholes, and tie a few square knots in the threads. Wind a small amount of gray roving around the threads and needle felt it. Then tie a little puff of black roving on the end of the TAIL and cut off the excess threads.

We all know who the real star of the show is...

9 To create the TORCH, wind orange roving around one end of the 3-inch (7.6 cm) black chenille stem and lightly felt it in place. Pull the fibers up and away from the chenille so they look like flames.

10 Create a riser for your elephant following the steps on page 64. Stand the elephant on a wool riser, and sew him in place with a double thickness of black embroidery floss, so that the stitches look like shoelaces. Hide the starting knot under one shoe and sink the other knot underneath the riser. If you like, cover the knot with a bit of yellow wool and needle felt over it.

Sideshow Banner

What better background for the stars of the show? Guaranteed to set the stage and attract attention.

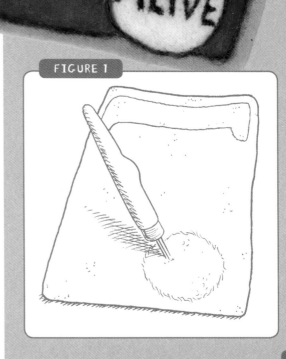

Finished Size
5 x 8 inches (12.7 x 20.3 cm)

Materials & Tools
Felting needles: 38 and 40 gauge
Foam felting mat
Yellow, orange, red, white, and blue roving
Multi-needle tool

1 Draw a 5 x 8-inch (12.7 x 20.3 cm) rectangle on your foam surface, and lay out the orange wool roving in a shingled pattern. Make the **BASE** with two layers of the orange roving, one horizontal and one vertical. Using a multi-needle tool, needle felt the orange roving very well until it lies flat. This will involve turning the whole piece over a few times so the wool doesn't stick into the foam. Add fiber to any thin spots.

2 Working now mainly on one side, add the yellow **BANNER** across the top, the red curtains, and the white circle (fig. 1). With thin strips of the blue roving, outline the whole banner and add the writing. Felt over the whole piece to blend and even out the surface.

FIGURE 1

Sweet SHOPPE

Do you have a (felt) sweet tooth? Satisfy the craving with donuts, truffles, cupcakes, and more. Just be warned: these treats really do look good enough to eat!

Created by Yin Chan

World's Finest Truffle

With the help from your cookie cutter, this creamy and elegant chocolate is easy to make and delicious to behold. Add different details to make other special truffles.

Finished Size
1 inch (2.5 cm)

Materials & Tools
Felting needle: 40 gauge
Foam felting mat
Dark brown, pink, and red roving
Cookie cutter
Ruler or measuring tape

1 Stuff the dark brown roving inside the cookie cutter. Place the cookie cutter on the felting mat and felt the roving down using a size 40 needle. Take care not to push the needle all the way through.

2 Keep felting until the top is firm, carefully turn the cookie cutter over, and repeat the same process until the bottom side is also firm.

3 Take the shape out from the cookie cutter and measure the height of it. If you'd like a thicker layer, carefully put the felt back inside the cookie cutter and add more layers.

TIP: *It's especially important to maintain a uniform height for all of your chocolates when you are planning to create a chocolate box set.*

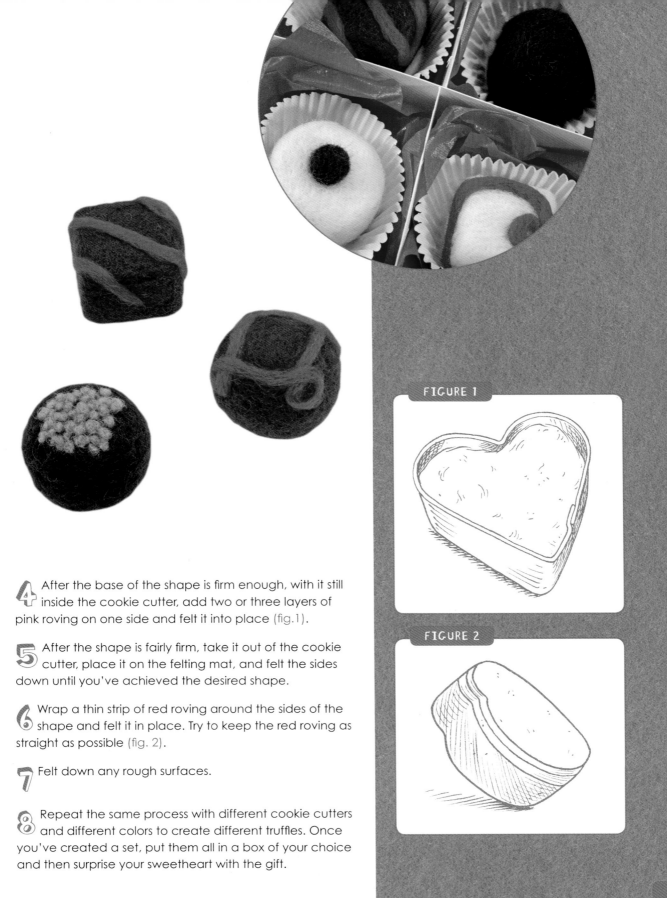

4 After the base of the shape is firm enough, with it still inside the cookie cutter, add two or three layers of pink roving on one side and felt it into place (fig.1).

5 After the shape is fairly firm, take it out of the cookie cutter, place it on the felting mat, and felt the sides down until you've achieved the desired shape.

6 Wrap a thin strip of red roving around the sides of the shape and felt it in place. Try to keep the red roving as straight as possible (fig. 2).

7 Felt down any rough surfaces.

8 Repeat the same process with different cookie cutters and different colors to create different truffles. Once you've created a set, put them all in a box of your choice and then surprise your sweetheart with the gift.

FIGURE 1

FIGURE 2

Fresh Strawberry Cupcake

Made with an actual cupcake pan, this delectable treat "bakes" up quickly. Customize the frosting for endless variations.

Finished Size

2 inches (5.1 cm) in diameter

Materials & Tools

Felting needles: 40 and 42 gauge
Foam felting mat
Light brown and pink roving (for the cupcake)
Red, pink, white, and green roving (for the strawberry)
Dark brown roving (for the chocolate heart)
Cupcake pan
Heart-shaped cookie cutter

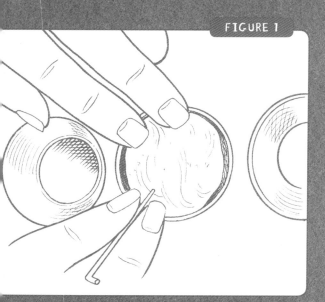

FIGURE 1

1 To create the **CUPCAKE BASE**, wrap the strips of light brown roving into a ball shape, stuff it inside the cupcake pan, and felt it down using a size 40 needle. Take care not to push the needle all the way through to the cupcake pan as this could break the needle (fig. 1).

2 Keep needle felting the top of the cupcake until it's fairly firm. Carefully take the base out from the cupcake pan, place it on the felting mat and felt down the bottom and the sides of the shape until fairly firm. Continue adding and felting the light brown roving until you've achieved the desired cupcake shape and size.

3 Wrap the pink roving on top of the cupcake and felt it into place to create frosting. Continue to add three or four layers of pink roving to create a thick frosting and felt it down until the top of the cupcake is nicely covered.

4 To create the **STRAWBERRY**, wrap some red roving into a pinecone shape and felt it using a size 40 needle. Keep felting the red roving until it's firm.

5 Once you've got a nice pinecone shape, felt one side of the strawberry down into a flatter surface. This will be the cut side of the strawberry. Using a size 42 needle, carefully felt the pink roving down on the flat side. Work from the center of the felt out to create a pink layer, though leave some of the red felt showing around the edge.

6 Add a thin strip of white roving in the middle of pink roving.

7 To create the **LEAF**, place some green roving on the felting mat and felt it into a pebble shape using a size 42 needle. Attach the leaf to the top of the strawberry.

8 To create the **CHOCOLATE HEART**, stuff the brown roving inside your cookie cutter, place the cookie cutter on the felting mat, and felt it down using a size 40 needle until it's firm. Carefully turn the cookie cutter over and repeat the same process until the bottom side is also firm.

9 Carefully take the shape out of the cookie cutter, and needle felt around the sides. If desired, felt more layers of brown roving around the shape to make it larger.

10 To add the decorations, felt a bit of white roving in the center of the pink frosting on the cupcake. This will be the cream for your toppings and act as a base.

11 Using a size 40 needle, carefully felt the strawberry in place on the white roving.

12 Place the chocolate heart behind the strawberry and felt it in place securely. Felt any remaining rough areas until they're smooth. Now enjoy your fresh cupcake with a nice cup of tea!

Customize your cupcakes for special holiday celebrations.

Mint Chocolate Frosted Donut

Go ahead... indulge in a delicious mint chocolate (felted) donut! Add sprinkles, fillings, or other toppings for your favorite flavor.

Finished Size
1¾ inches (4.4 cm) in diameter

Materials & Tools
Felting needles: 40 and 42 gauges
Foam felting mat
Brown, golden brown, green, and
  dark brown roving
Pen or pencil

FIGURE 1

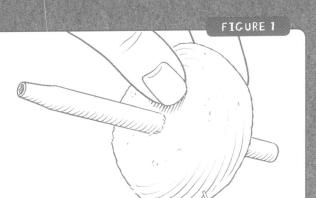

1 Form the **DONUT BASE** by wrapping strips of brown roving around a pen to create a disc, and carefully felt around the side of the disc with a size 40 felting needle. Take care not to push the needle all the way through to the pen as this may break the needle. Continue wrapping and turning the felt while felting it to create a round disc (fig. 1).

2 With the pen or pencil still in the center, place the disc on the felting mat and felt down the top until it's firm and smooth. Carefully turn the disc over and repeat the same process until the bottom side is also firm.

3 After the disc is firm on both sides, remove the pen or pencil and carefully felt around the donut hole. Insert the pen or pencil often to maintain the circular donut hole shape. Continue felting until the center is firm and round.

4. After the base of the donut is firm, you can start to add details. For the mint chocolate donut, wrap a thin strip of golden brown roving around the side of the donut. Using a size 42 needle, carefully felt the strip into place (fig. 2).

5. Lay a strip of green roving on the top side of the donut, trying not to cover the donut hole. Carefully felt the green roving onto top of the donut, adding layers until you have the desired thickness of the **FROSTING**.

6. Form a thin strip from your dark brown roving by rubbing the roving between your palms to make the **ICING**. Carefully drape the roving strip on top of the green frosting and felt lightly. Create the simple zigzag or your own design. If the strip is not long enough, add another roving strip to continue your design.

7. Continue to felt any rough surfaces as needed to create a smooth round shape. Pair your felt donut with a cup of coffee and enjoy!

FIGURE 2

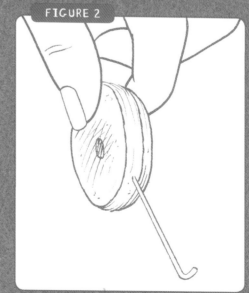

Orange & Cream Ice Pop

Refreshing sweet orange with a creamy filling—just the thing to help you stay cool during a hot summer!

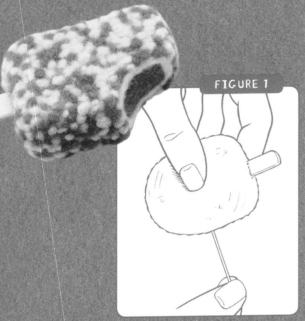

FIGURE 1

FIGURE 2

Finished Size
1½ x 3 inches (3.8 x 7.6 cm)

Materials & Tools
Felting needle: 40 gauge
Foam felting mat
Orange and white roving
Frozen pop stick
Glue

1 Form the creamy inside of the ice cream pop by wrapping strips of white roving around the stick. Leave around an inch (2.5 cm) of the stick uncovered at the base. Felt the white roving base into an ice cream pop shape with a size 40 needle, adding more white roving until you've achieved the desired size (fig. 1).

2 Wrap the white felt in orange roving, place it on the felting mat, and felt it until the orange roving covers the top and the sides of the white felt piece. The bottom of the white felt should be left uncovered and the orange roving should be about ⅓ inch (.8 cm) thickness on top of the white felt (fig. 2).

3 Take your time to check your ice cream pop. If there's any white roving shown underneath, add more orange roving to cover it up.

4 Carefully take the pop stick out, put some glue on the tip of the stick, and carefully insert it back into the ice cream pop.

5 Kick back, relax, and enjoy your refreshing treat under the hot sun.

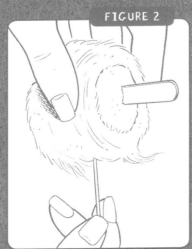

Rainbow Swirl Lollipop

You'll be a sucker for this simple felt chain "swirl" technique.

Finished Size
3 inches (7.6 cm) tall
Materials & Tools
Felting needle: 40 gauge
Foam felting mat
Multiple colors of roving
A spare felting needle of
    any size (optional)
Toothpick
Glue (optional)
Candy wrapper and
    ribbon (optional)

1 Form thin strips—or chains—from each color of roving by rubbing each of them between your palms. Each strip should be about 8 to 10 inches (20.3 to 25.4 cm) long. Place all the strips on the felting mat, and arrange the colors side by side (fig. 1).

2 With a spare felting needle, pin one end of the strips onto the felting mat, and slowly twist all of the strips together to create a big strip.

TIP: *You may have a difficult time if you're trying to twist too many strips together. If needed, use another spare felting needle to pin down the middle section of the strips to hold them in place. Twisting the strips slowly may also be helpful.*

3 With the end still pinned onto the felting foam, slowly roll up the twisted strip to form a disc (fig. 2).

4 Place the disc on the felting mat. Using a size 40 needle, carefully felt the end of the twisted strip into the side of the disc until it begins to felt in place.

5 Continue to felt around the sides of the disc shape. Push the needle through to the center of the disc to securely felt the twisted strip into the disc. Once the disc is secured, carefully insert the toothpick into the side of the lollipop.

TIP: *For this step, you can use glue on the toothpick, but be careful: the glue can stain the lollipop felt.*

6 Place your rainbow-swirl lollipop inside a candy wrapper and tie a ribbon. You're done.

FIGURE 1

FIGURE 2

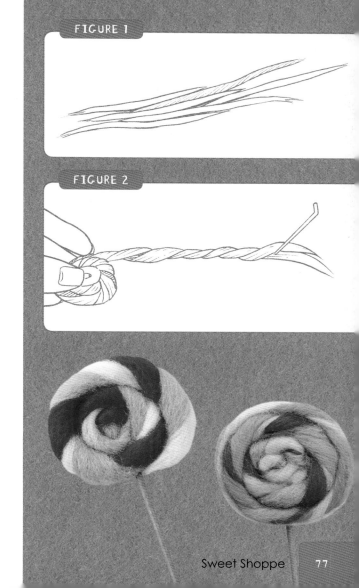

Silly Science Lab

Welcome to the Science Lab, where we're testing the frontiers of needle felting. Grab your tools and let the felt experiments commence!

Created by Michelle Kiker

Scientist

This ambitious scientist hopes to someday take over the world. Or at least make some friends to help her with the lab work.

Finished Size
1½ x 3¾ inches (3.8 x 9.5 cm)

Materials & Tools
Felting needle
Foam felting mat
Polyester fiberfill
White, gray, peach, pink, black, light brown, turquoise, and dark purple roving
Chopstick, pencil, or thin dowel
Scissors

1 Create a **BODY** base out of polyester fiberfill. Fold and felt a portion of polyester fiberfill into a tapered, cone-like shape.

2 To create a base for the **HEAD**, fold and felt a second piece of polyester fiberfill into a small sphere, approximately half the size of the body base.

3 Cover the body base in white wool roving to create the scientist's **LAB COAT**. Felt the roving into the base until you've created a smooth texture and no fiberfill is visible.

4 Create the illusion of **PANTS** by needle felting gray felt around the base of the figure, covering the white roving. Continue felting this area until it is slightly recessed to add dimension.

5 Portion out a long piece of white wool roving for one **ARM**. Designate one end of the chopstick or dowel the "shoulder." Wrap the length of white roving around it and felt it slightly to secure, starting from the shoulder end. Wrap a length that measures approximately half the length of the body.

6 After wrapping, felt gently to bind fibers together. Continue to add fiber and needle felt.

7 Wrap a small piece of black wool roving around the **HAND** end and felt the fiber until it attaches to the white roving (fig. 1). Continue felting until the gloved hand is defined.

8 Slide the arm off the dowel carefully. Felt the black wool roving to close the hole left by the dowel, rounding off the hand.

9 Repeat to create the second arm.

10 Hold or pin the arm to the top of the cone body and needle felt to secure (fig. 2). Attach one arm to each side of the body. Use your fingers to bend the arms into the desired pose, or felt them to the base.

11 Cover the head base completely with peach wool roving. Felt the roving until it adheres to the polyester fiberfill, and continue needle felting until it's smooth.

12 To create the **HAIR**, portion out a length of light brown roving and begin to loosely felt it into the peach roving on the head. Leaving a square area uncovered on the front for the face, sculpt the hair into the desired style, adding extra roving if necessary to create volume. Leave the ends loose, using scissors to cut off extra length and shape as desired.

13 Portion out small pieces of black roving for **EYES**. Roll the small pieces between your fingers to create small oval balls of equal size. Using a single needle, felt the black roving until it adheres to the face. Shape the eyes until they're smooth and slightly recessed into the face.

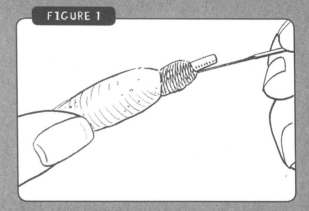

FIGURE 1

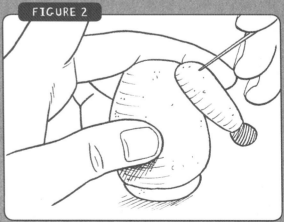

FIGURE 2

Hello, robot friend!

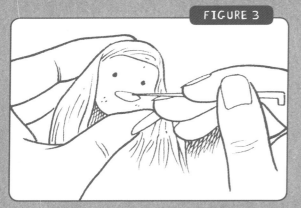

FIGURE 3

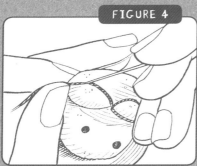

FIGURE 4

14 Needle felt white roving into the half circle shape until it adheres smoothly to the face to create the **MOUTH**. Sculpt into a smile, or a smirk! Felt the edges of the mouth to create definition and finish (fig. 3).

15 Portion out small pieces of pink roving for the **CHEEK** highlights. Roll the pieces between your fingers to create small oval balls of equal size. Using a single needle, felt the pink roving until it adheres to the face, slightly beneath each eye.

16 To create the **GOGGLES**, portion out a small piece of turquoise roving. Needle felt the turquoise roving into the top front of the head, covering the front of the hair. Sculpt two circles that will serve as the lenses for the goggles. Create larger circles to make a larger, more whimsical set of goggles, or create smaller circles for a more realistic shape.

17 Using a small portion of dark purple roving, felt around the two turquoise circles to create a rim for the goggles (fig. 4). Continue felting to create definition on the turquoise glass and the purple rim.

18 Press the head shape onto the body shape at the desired angle. Felt carefully up through the body and down through the head until the two are securely attached.

Robot

What's a science lab without a trusty robot assistant? Personalize your felt robot with buttons, accessories, maybe even a bow tie!

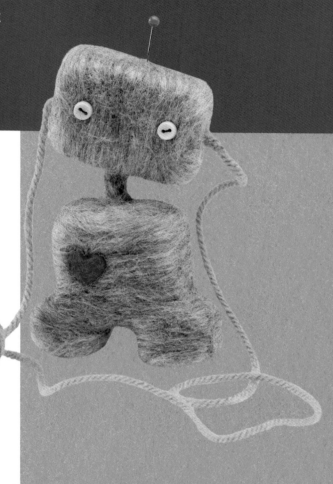

Finished Size
4 x 2½ inches (10.2 x 6.4 cm)

Materials & Tools
Felting needle
Foam felting mat
Polyester fiberfill*
Gray** and red roving
Gray craft felt
Gray yarn
Sewing needle
Black thread
2 buttons, white (for eyes)
Scissors
Sewing pin, size 24, in red (for antenna)
Craft glue
*You'll need 1 ounce (28 grams).
**You'll need ½ ounce (14 grams) of this color.

1. Using a portion of polyester fiberfill, sculpt a rectangular shape for the **HEAD**.

2. Portion out a second, slightly smaller piece of polyester fiberfill for the **BODY**. Fold and felt the fiber to create a square shape, and then add additional fiber to create two smaller squares at the base of the figure that will be the **LEGS**. Take care to leave a space between the two legs (fig. 1).

3. Fold and felt a small piece of polyester fiberfill to create a third, half-sphere shape. This will be the robot's **PLUG** (fig. 1). Sculpt one flat side that will become the base for the plug prongs.

FIGURE 1

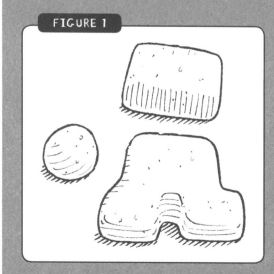

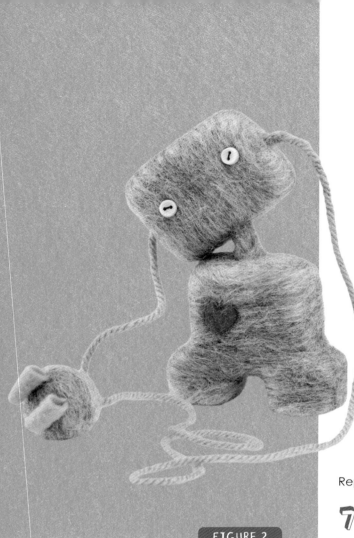

4 Using gray wool roving, cover all three shapes completely until no polyester fiberfill is visible. Felt the fiber until smooth.

5 Portion out a small piece of red wool roving. Needle felt the fiber into the gray wool roving to create a flat **HEART** shape, sculpting a pointed bottom and an indented top. Continue to felt until the fiber is smooth and the heart can be clearly seen.

6 Using a needle and a small length of black thread, attach the button **EYES** to the head. Knot one end of the thread and push the needle through the back of the head to the front, attaching the button and pushing the needle back through the head. Repeat once or twice until the button is secure. Repeat for the second button eye.

7 Portion out a piece of gray wool roving and place it over any black threads visible on the back of the head. Felt in place.

8 Cut two small, identical rectangles from the gray craft felt. These will be the **PRONGS** for the plug. Fold one of the felt rectangles in half. Press both ends together and press them against the flat end of the plug. Felt the rectangle ends until they adhere to the wool roving (fig. 2), making sure to secure each end.

9 Repeat for second rectangle, placing it parallel to the first.

10 Portion out a small piece of gray wool roving. Fold and needle felt the roving together to create a small, semi-rectangular piece that will connect the robot's head and body. Felt until the piece is somewhat thick, but it does not need to be stiff.

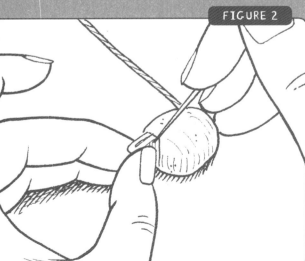

FIGURE 2

11 Felt and attach one end of the connector to the middle of the head. Felt the other end of the connector to the top of the body piece until it adheres to the gray wool roving.

12 Continue to felt both attached ends until they are secure. The head might be a little heavy and cause the neck to bend to the side. If you like, adding additional fiber to the connector can stiffen it enough to hold the head up.

13 Cut a length of yarn; the length is up to you, but it is better to be too long than too short. Hold one end of the yarn against one side of the head and felt until it adheres securely to the gray roving.

14 Leaving a length of yarn long enough so that the plug will sit comfortably on the table, press the thread across the rounded top of the plug shape and felt it until it adheres securely.

15 Wrap the remaining yarn around the body as many times as possible or desired.

16 Hold the second end of the yarn to the other side of the head and needle felt it until it adheres securely to the gray roving.

17 Finally, push the sewing pin into the top of the head to create the robot's ANTENNA. If necessary, add a small dot of craft glue to the pointed end of the pin before pressing it in to secure it within the head.

Urp... that beaker juice was fizzy and delicious!

Carnivorous Plant

Careful: this mutant plant has quite an appetite … and lots of personalities!

Finished Size
4½ inches (11.4 cm) tall

Materials & Tools
Template (page 127)
Felting needle
Foam felting mat
Scissors
Chenille stem, 1 or 2, any color
Light green, pink, red, white, and brown roving
Polyester fiberfill
Green craft felt
Black thread
Sewing needle
6 seed beads, black
Small terra cotta planter

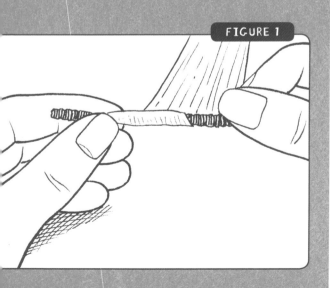

FIGURE 1

1 Cut three equal lengths of chenille stem that will serve as the STEMS for the plants.

2 Portion out a piece of light green wool roving. Designate one end of a chenille stem segment the HEAD. Starting from the other end, wrap the light green wool roving around the chenille stem and needle felt slightly to secure (fig. 1). Continue wrapping and adding fiber up the length of the chenille stem, increasing the number of layers as you work up to the head end.

3 Continue to add fiber and felt until the chenille stem is no longer visible. Wrap the green roving around the head end, adding volume until it begins to look like a sphere or a lollipop (fig. 2). After wrapping, felt gently to bind the fibers together tightly until smooth.

4 Repeat with the remaining two chenille stem segments.

5 Working with a length of black thread, press the needle through the bottom of the head about halfway between where you would like the EYES positioned, and angle toward the eye position. The eyes should be positioned on the top front of the head. Place one seed bead on the thread, and press the needle back through the head. Try to keep stitches close to each other; this will make hiding them easier.

6 Attach the second eye, press the needle back through the head, tie off, and cut off the excess thread. Position a small piece of light green roving over any exposed thread ends and needle felt in place.

7 Using a small portion of red felt, create a MOUTH by sculpting a line, a half circle, or a triangle shape along the front of the head (fig. 3). Felt the red wool roving into head until it adheres to the face and is slightly recessed to create dimension.

8 Felt one or two pieces of white wool roving into the red roving to create pointed TEETH.

9 Portion out small pieces of pink roving for the CHEEK highlights. Roll the pieces between your fingers to create small oval balls of equal size. Using a single needle, felt the pink roving until it adheres to the face, slightly beneath each eye.

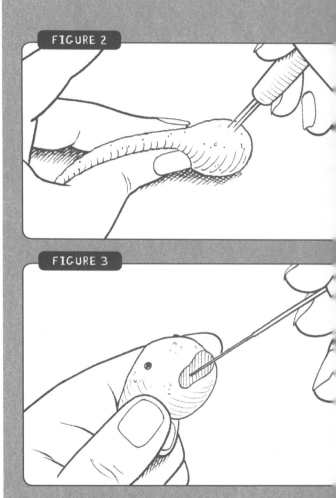

FIGURE 2

FIGURE 3

10 Repeat for each head. Create a different face for each head to give them fun personalities!

11 Bend the bottom stem of each piece, and place the three plants stem-first into the flowerpot. Using polyester fiberfill, fill in the bottom half of the flowerpot, pressing around the stems until they are almost securely packed and can stand on their own. Felt the fiberfill gently until it adheres lightly to itself.

12 Portion out some of the brown wool roving and fill in the rest of the flowerpot. Felt gently until it adheres to the polyester fiberfill and there is no white showing. Continue to add fiber and felt until the stems can stand strongly on their own.

13 Carefully use your fingers to shape and curve the plant stems so that the heads sit at different levels to create a more dimensional figure.

14 Using the **LEAF** template and the green craft felt, cut out four leaf shapes.

15 Needle felt the leaves to the stems where desired to create a good balance (fig. 4). Attach the leaves directly to the plant stem, or near where the stem meets the brown roving. Be sure to needle felt gently, but attach the leaves securely.

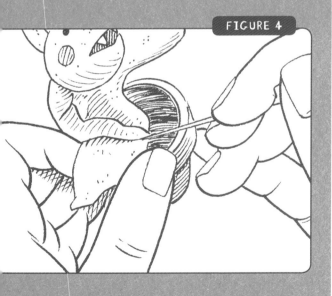

FIGURE 4

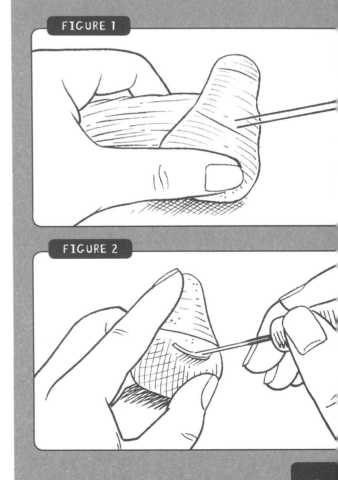

Beakers

Beakers are a must-have in any science lab. Create bubbles or swirls, depending on the felt concoction.

Finished Size
2 x 2½ inches (5.1 x 6.4 cm)

Materials & Tools
Felting needle
Foam felting mat
Polyester fiberfill
White, black, red, and green roving

1 Create a **BASE** out of polyester fiberfill. Fold and felt a portion of polyester fiberfill into a tapered, cone-like shape with sloping sides. Felt the fiberfill until it is sturdy and firm.

2 Cover the fiberfill base completely with white wool roving and felt the roving to the base (fig. 1).

3 Needle felt a portion of red or green wool roving around the bottom of the shape until it adheres to the white roving to create the contents of the beaker. Add fiber until the white roving is covered completely.

4 To create a simple beaker, felt the colored roving into a flat, level band around the bottom. To create a beaker with bubbling, active contents, sculpt the colored roving into a wavy line. To create **BUBBLES**, roll small pieces of roving into balls with your fingers and carefully felt them until they adhere to the white roving, sculpting them into the desired shape.

5 Portion out three or four small pieces of black roving. Pull and roll each piece between your fingers to create a line of fiber.

6 Using a single felting needle, felt each black fiber line on the main shape to create **MEASUREMENT MARKINGS** on the side of the beaker at even intervals (fig. 2).

FIGURE 1

FIGURE 2

Brain in Jar

Felt scientists are required to have at least one felt brain on display. Use clear thread to suspend the brain so that it looks like it's floating in liquid.

Finished Size
2½ x 1½ x 2 inches (6.4 x 3.8 x 5.1 cm)

Materials & Tools
Felting needle
Foam felting mat
Polyester fiberfill*
Light pink and dark pink roving
Clear thread, fishing line, or elastic thread
Sewing needle
Glue gun
Clear jar with lid, any size
*You'll need 1 ounce (28 grams).

1 Using a piece of polyester fiberfill, create an oblong, egglike shape. Fold and felt the fiberfill until it reaches the desired shape. Make sure that this shape is able to fit through the opening of the jar you have chosen.

2 Create the basic brain shape by sculpting a line into the top of the brain, dividing the oblong base into two halves (fig. 1). Continue the line around onto the bottom of the core; it should bisect the entire shape.

3 Sculpt two angled lines into the core, beginning on the bottom of the shape and running as if to cross the line created in step 2. Sculpt these lines halfway up the shape, stopping before they reach the line from step 2.

4 Add an additional portion of polyester fiberfill to the back base of the core, creating a small, defined lump. Sculpt a line to divide this lump into two halves, continuing the line dividing the top of the main form.

5 Cover the base with light pink wool roving. Continue to felt and add fiber until no fiberfill is visible and the shape is smooth.

6 Portion out some small pieces of dark pink wool roving. Roll each piece between your fingers to create short, threadlike lengths of fiber.

7 Begin to add details by needle felting these lengths of dark pink wool roving into the recesses (fig. 2) to create an appearance of added depth.

8 Continue to lightly needle felt lengths of dark pink roving into swirls on the light pink roving, creating a brainy look. Needle felt until smooth.

9 Cut a length of clear thread approximately three quarters of the length of the jar. Tie a strong knot on one end, thread the needle, and press it carefully through the brain shape, starting on the bottom and pressing up through the center. Remove the needle from the thread.

10 Using a small amount of hot glue, attach the thread end securely to the bottom center of the jar lid.

11 Wait for the glue to dry completely. Carefully lower the brain through the jar opening and attach the lid!

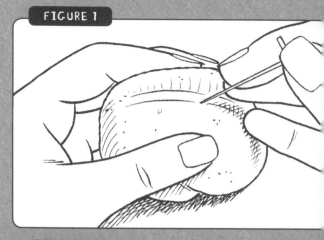

FIGURE 1

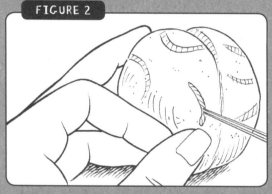

FIGURE 2

Created by Aimee Ray

Wooly
WOODLAND

Ah, a fresh felted forest glade and a few welcoming friends: the perfect needle-felted outing.

Finished Size
2 inches (5.1 cm) tall

Materials & Tools
Templates (page 127)
Felting needle
Foam felting mat
Brown*, dark brown, light brown,
   and moss green roving
Light green and dark green wool
   craft felt
Embroidery needle
Green, brown, and pink
   embroidery floss
Scissors
Fiberfill
*You'll need ½ ounce (14 grams)
   of this color.

Tree Stump
Craft felt leaves and embroi-
dered grass and flowers make
unique embellishments for this
felted tree stump, some little
creature's cozy home.

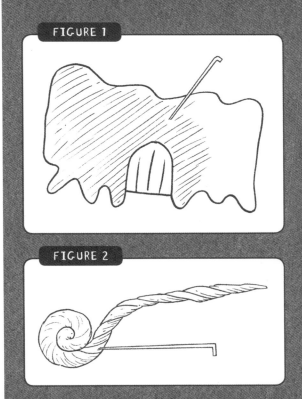

FIGURE 1

FIGURE 2

1 Use the **STUMP** template as a guide to create a flat brown shape that will become the tree stump (fig. 1). Make it ¼ inch (.6 cm) thick.

2 Felt the **DOOR** from dark brown roving and attach it to the stump to create a doorway.

3 Felt a tapering **BRANCH** shape and attach it to the side of the stump.

4 Felt the top of the stump by twisting and felting light brown roving into a long rope and then rolling this into a coil, attaching the rope to itself and adding to the length of the rope as you go (fig. 2). Make this circular piece about 1½ inches (3.8 cm) across.

FIGURE 3

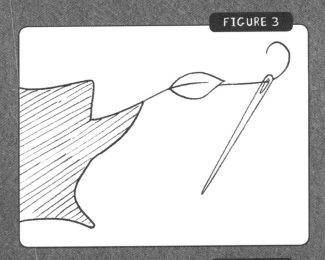

FIGURE 4

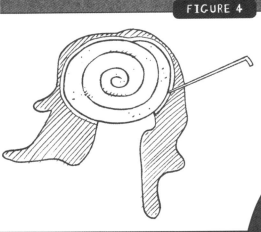

5 Embroider **FLOWERS** and **VINES** on the stump and lines on the door using the stitch pattern and photo as a guide. Cut and attach two light green craft felt **LEAVES** to the end of the branch by running floss through the length of the branch, through the leaf, and then back again (fig. 3), tying a knot on the backside.

6 Curl the tree shape into a tube and felt the back edges together, attaching the top coil piece in place (fig. 4). Stuff a bit of fiberfill inside to help hold its shape.

7 Using the template, cut a piece of light green felt for the **BASE** and six dark green leaves. Center the stump on the base and felt it in place, bending the roots out so it will sit flatly. Felt thin layers of moss green roving around the roots.

8 Stitch the leaves in place and embroider grass onto the base around the roots.

Mushrooms

What makes mushrooms so magically irresistible, especially in felt? To help them stand, felt the stems to a craft felt base.

Finished Size
1 inch (2.5 cm) tall

Materials & Tools
Felting needle
Foam felting mat
White, pink, red, and moss green roving
Light green and dark green wool felt
Scissors
Green embroidery floss
Embroidery needle

1 To create the **CAP**, make a flat disk shape from red roving, about ½ inch (1.3 cm) wide. Felt white spots on the top.

2 For the **STEM**, make a ½ x ¼-inch (1.3 x .6 cm) cylinder from white roving and attach it to the bottom of the red piece (fig. 1).

3 Make an egg shape from pink roving about ¾ inch (1.9 cm) tall. Flatten one end and make the other end a rounded point. Felt white spots in place. Repeat step 2 for the stem.

4 Cut a piece of light green felt for the **BASE** and felt the mushrooms to it. Felt thin layers of moss green roving around the mushroom bases (fig. 2).

5 Cut three dark green felt **LEAVES**, and stitch them in place to the base. Embroider green grass around the moss and mushrooms.

FIGURE 1

FIGURE 2

Squirrel

Make your own friendly forest forager, complete with a loose, fluffy tail.

Finished Size
1¼ inches (3.2 cm) tall

Materials & Tools
Felting needle
Foam felting mat
Brown, dark brown, and light brown roving

1 Felt a peanut shape that measures 1¼ inches (3.2 cm) tall from brown roving. Create an indent to define the **HEAD** and **BODY**: make the head section about half the size of the body section.

2 Felt an oval shaped layer of light brown roving to the belly of the squirrel's body.

3 Take a small amount of brown roving and fold it in half three or four times. Roll it between your fingers, and shape it into a tiny **ARM** for the squirrel (fig. 1). Felt it in place on the squirrel's body. Create the other arm and two **FEET** shapes, and attach them to the body.

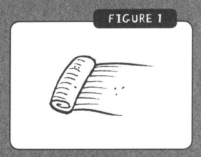

FIGURE 1

Must find more (felted) acorns!

4 Roll two brown pieces half the length of the arms and attach them to the squirrel's head for **EARS**.

5 Roll two tiny bits of dark brown roving between your fingers to create **EYES** for the squirrel (fig. 2). Felt these in place on either side of the head.

6 For the **TAIL**, pull off small amounts of brown roving and lay them together, forming points at either end. Create a firm tuft about 4 inches (10.2 cm) long, but don't felt it. Fold this piece in half and twist the two pointed ends together, forming a tail shape (fig. 3). Felt the flat end a bit to hold it together and attach this end to the base of the squirrel.

FIGURE 2

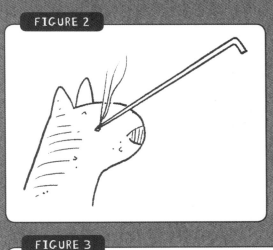

FIGURE 3

Acorn

Sweet treat to all kinds of forest creatures, felt acorns are a snap to make; create several in different shapes or shades of browns or greens.

Finished Size
1¼ inches (3.2 cm) tall

Materials & Tools
Felting needle
Foam felting mat
Brown and light brown roving

1 Felt a ball from light brown roving, and make one end pointed to create the **SHELL** of the acorn. Make the acorn about ¾ inch (1.9 cm) long.

2 For the **CAP**, felt a flat disk shape from brown roving a little larger around than the acorn bottom and attach it to the top end. Wrap more brown roving around the top and felt it in place.

3 Make a small **STEM** for the cap by rolling brown roving between your fingers and felting it firmly into shape. Attach it to the top of the acorn cap.

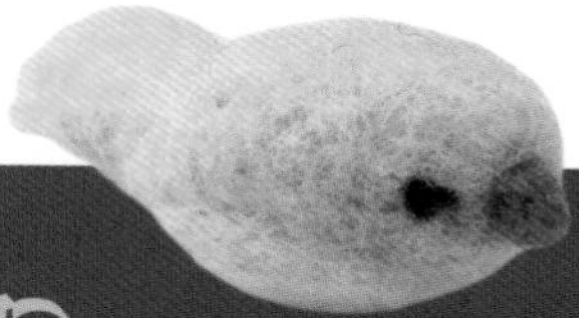

Robin

Made with just a few tufts of roving, this tiny bird perches happily on the edge of the tree stump.

Finished Size
1¼ x 1 inch (3.2 x 2.5 cm)

Materials & Tools
Felting needle
Foam felting mat
Dark brown, brown, cream, and pink roving

1 Felt an egg shape 1 inch (2.5 cm) long from pink roving. Add a flat, rounded **TAIL** shape to one end (fig. 1).

2 Felt an oval of cream roving to the bottom of the bird shape to make a **CHEST** and **BELLY**.

3 Roll a bit of brown roving between your fingers to make a little **BEAK** shape and felt it in place on the bird's face (fig. 2).

4 Roll two tiny bits of dark brown roving between your fingers to create **EYES** for the bird. Felt these in place on either side of the beak.

FIGURE 1

FIGURE 2

Created by Chrissy Mahuna

PIRATE ISLAND

What's a deserted felt island without a super-sized crab, a pirate skull, and a treasure map? Throw in a lush palm tree, and all that's missing is some needle-felted refreshment!

Crab

This surly little crab
has legs you can pose,
thanks to his wire armatures.

Finished Size
3½ x 7 x 5 inches (8.9 x 17.8 x 12.7 cm)

Materials & Tools
Templates (page 124)
Felting needle: 38 gauge
Foam felting mat
Core wool stuffing*
Red, white, and black wool roving
Black wool yarn
Tiny tufts of yellow wool roving
Red and white craft felt
Scissors
⅛-inch-wide (.3 cm) wire
Wire cutters
Glue gun
*You'll need ½ ounce (14 grams).

1 Loosely needle felt the core wool stuffing into the shape of a **CRAB SHELL** about 6 inches (15.2 cm) long. Keep the middle of the body super puffy, while thinning it out toward the pointy ends.

2 Felt the red wool roving onto the shell, but just onto one side. Needle felt the white wool roving onto the bottom, leaving a distinct line between the red and white wool. As you apply the white roving, start to define the belly area by felting down the pointy outside areas to leave a puffy circle in the center. Create two semi-circle lines that split the top center area (which will become the face) and follow the curves of the puffy center circle (which will become the start of the legs). Divide the semi-circle crescents into five lumpy balls on each side. Start by felting the lines to divide the crescent, then go back and tighten up the wool by shaping it into circular balls (figs. 1–3).

3 Using a sharp pair of pointy scissors, cut a 2-inch-long (5.1 cm) by ½-inch-deep (1.3 cm) cut along the red and white seam line at the center front of the shell. To create the **EYES**, felt two small puffy balls of black wool roving, smaller than marbles, and insert them into the eye sockets. Felt around the outside edge of the eyes to secure them in place.

4 Once the eyes are in place, needle felt the ridges on the front of the shell. These will help create an **EYEBROW** area. Felt an indented line along the front of the shell about an inch (2.5 cm) back, then divide that ridge down the center and continue to divide out towards the pointy ends. Felt tiny white accent dots in the center of each ridge.

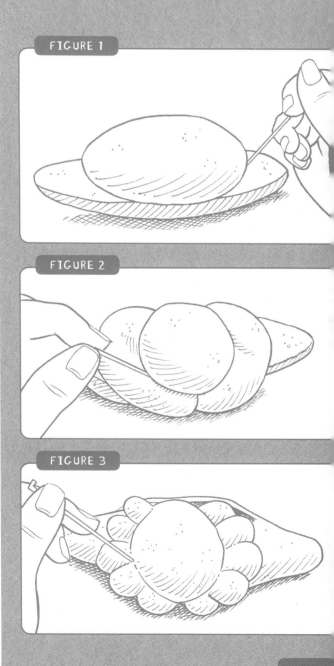

FIGURE 1

FIGURE 2

FIGURE 3

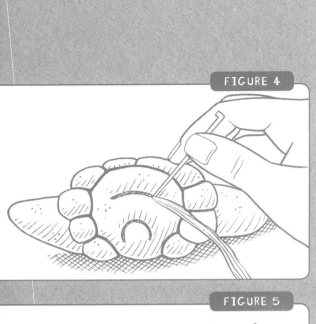

FIGURE 4

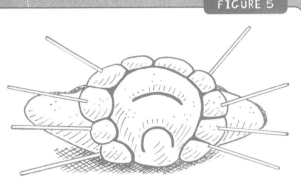

FIGURE 5

5 Split the black wool yarn in half, and use it to felt an outline around the red shell and white belly seams. Also, felt the yarn around each leg ball, and add a couple of lines in the ridges (fig. 4).

6 Using your scissors, cut into the belly from the back leg ball through to the leg ball across from it. Be careful to cut a small hole only through the inside of the crab; you don't want to accidentally cut the whole thing open. Repeat the cut for each leg ball except for the first pair, which is part of the face.

7 To make the **LEGS**, cut three pieces of thick wire the length of the crab's shell and two wires that are half the length of the shell using wire cutters. Thread each of the longer wires through the lower three leg ball cuts. You might have to wiggle the wire a little to get it through. Insert each of the shorter wires into the leg balls that are second from the front: These will become the claws (fig. 5).

8 Trace and cut out six of the leg template shapes from the red craft felt. Felt tiny white balls down the middle of the leg shapes for accent spots, and trim the fuzzy wool off the back of the red felt. With the belly facing up, squirt a line of hot glue onto the wire, and fold and hold the leg in half around the wire. Trim any extra glue that may have come out along the seam. Tuck the ends of the craft felt into the hole that was cut for the wire. You can lightly needle felt the joint to help secure the leg to the body.

9 Trace and cut out four **CLAW** template shapes from the red craft felt and two **THUMB** shapes from the white craft felt. Felt a tuft of red wool roving on the outside of each of the four claw patterns leaving some fluffy wool overlapping the outside edge of the pattern. Place two claws back-to-back and needle felt around the outside edge. Be sure to not needle felt in the middle; you'll need to keep it open for the wire to be inserted. Once the red wool roving is securely felted around the outer edge, add a few white spots and needle felt the flat end of the white thumb onto the inside of the claw. Thread the claws onto the two shorter wires and stuff the ends into the hole cut into the body. Needle felt the joints to secure.

10 Trace and cut out two **FINS** from red craft felt. Felt these at the shell seam on the back, behind the last two legs.

11 Felt on the final details by rolling tiny tufts of wool between your fingers to create accent spots. Add some yellow and black spots to the top of the shell, give the crab some life with highlights in his eyes, and even add some funny personality with angry eyebrows and a mustache.

I'm feeling a bit crabby today...

Pirate Skull

Arrgghh—it looks like this felt scallywag has lost his treasure and his tooth!

Finished Size
6 x 4 x 5 inches (15.2 x 10.2 x 12.7 cm)

Materials & Tools
Felting needle: 38 gauge
Foam felting mat
Core wool stuffing*
White and black roving
Black wool yarn
Black craft felt
Small tufts of red and blue roving
Scissors
*You'll need 1 ounce (28 grams).

FIGURE 1

1 To start the **SKULL**, loosely needle felt the core wool stuffing into a sphere that's a little bigger than a softball to use as the general base for the skull. Add a loosely felted egg shape to the bottom of the sphere to create a flattened area that will become the face (fig. 1).

2 Start defining the basic shapes of the skull by either felting indentations or adding small tufts of core wool onto the base. Here are a few elements you'll want to shape: adding to the cheek and brow bones, felting in the temples around the eyes, and taking in the teeth under the cheeks and at the base of the skull.

3 Using a sharp pair of scissors, cut a ½-inch-deep (1.3 cm) horizontal line where the **EYE SOCKETS** will be (fig. 2) and a vertical line where the **NASAL CAVITY** will be.

4 Put your fingers into the socket cut, and widen the hole—to about golf-ball size—by pushing the wool apart. Felt the core wool deeper into the hole and around the inside edges.

5 Needle felt a layer of white wool roving over the entire skull. You can start to give your skull more character at this point by playing with the placement of the eyebrows, by adding more wool to emphasize the cheek bones, or enlarging the eyes to give the skull more personality.

6 Felt the black yarn into vertical lines of the **TEETH** first, then to go back and attach them together. Start at the middle of the teeth, felt a short line down and around the bottom of the tooth area (fig. 3). To connect the tops of the teeth, start at one end and felt the black yarn from line to line with rounded shapes. Black out one of the front teeth to give the skull an authentic pirate look.

7 Fill in the eye and nose sockets by felting in some black wool roving. You can also give your skull some shading by blending some white and a little black wool roving together and felting it into the recessed areas.

8 To make the **EYEPATCH**, cut two 12-inch-long (30.5 cm) thin strips and a round half-circle patch that is a little bigger than one of the eye sockets out of black felt. You can felt small colored jewels like rubies, emeralds, or white pearls to decorate the patch if you'd like. Snip two small holes in the upper corners of the patch. Tie knots on one end of each felt strip, then thread through the holes. Wrap them around the skull and tie the strips in the back.

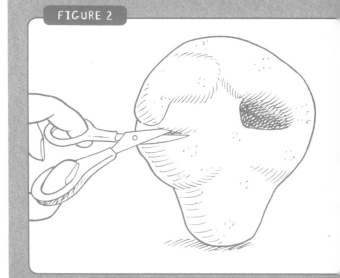

FIGURE 2

FIGURE 3

Palm Tree

No tropical island would be complete without at least one felt palm tree resting on a sandy base.

Finished Size
12 inches (13.5 cm) tall

Materials & Tools
Templates (page 125)
Felting needle: 38 gauge
Foam felting mat
Core wool stuffing
Tan, dark tan, and dark brown roving
Black wool yarn
Green, dark green, and tan craft felt
Wire cutters
¼-inch (.6 cm) thick wire (or other thick wire)
22-gauge wire (or thin craft wire)
Needle-nose pliers
Scissors
Glue gun
White craft glue (optional)
6-inch (15.2 cm) wooden disk (optional)
100 grit sand paper (optional)
Sand (optional)

1 Loosely felt an 8-inch-long (20.3 cm) tube shape out of the core wool stuffing, creating a thick, rounded **TRUNK** to help with stabilization. Loosely felt tan wool roving over the entire surface of the trunk.

2 Split strands of the black wool yarn in half. Divide the base into four points, and felt the ends of two strands of yarn to each point. One strand will spiral up the trunk in one direction and the other will spiral the opposite way to create the crisscross diamond pattern (fig. 1). To keep everything lined up, felt all eight strands at the same time as you work your way up the trunk, one crisscross at a time.

3 After the crisscross diamond pattern is finished, go back to shape and shade the diamonds. Felt the bottom of each diamond to make them look like they are overlapping each other. Add a tiny tuft of darker tan wool roving into the recess at the base of each diamond.

4 Using the wire cutters, cut the ¼-inch (.6 cm) wire about three times as long as the trunk. At a point that is slightly shorter than the length of the trunk, bend the wire at a 90° angle. Grab that point with the needle-nose pliers and bend the wire around the pliers in a flat spiral shape to create a sturdy base for the palm tree (fig. 2). Make sure the diameter of the spiraled wire base is smaller than the base of the trunk. Using a sharp pair of scissors, cut a small hole all the way up through the middle of the trunk. Insert the wire into the trunk and put a little hot glue on the underside of the wool to keep the wire in place.

5 Trace and cut out the **PALM LEAF** template shapes from green and dark green craft felt, and trace and cut out the **DEAD PALM LEAF** template shapes from tan craft felt. The number of leaves will determine how full your tree top is, so cut out as many as you'd like. Nine green leaves and four tan leaves is a good starting number.

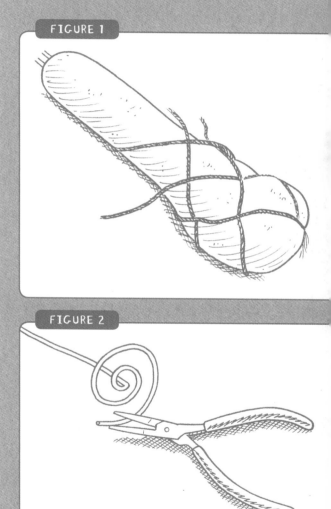

FIGURE 1

FIGURE 2

FIGURE 3

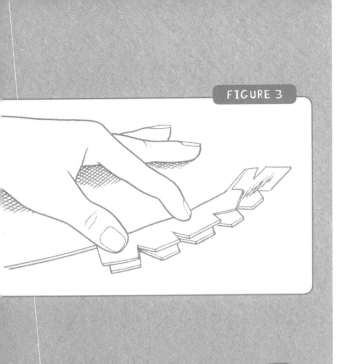

6 Trim the 22-gauge wire to approximately the length of the cutout leaves. Place the wire down the middle of one leaf, about halfway up the length of the leaf. Place a thin bead of hot glue on top of the wire, and quickly fold the entire leaf in half over it (fig. 3). Hold the felt in place for a few seconds until the hot glue is set. Open the leaf back up and bend the wire to create a nice and curvy palm frond branch. Repeat for each of the green and tan leaves.

7 Once all the leaves are attached to wires, start to arrange them together. Take four green leaves and twist the exposed wires all together. Then keep adding green leaves underneath by twisting the additional wires to the group. Save the tan leaves until last so they can hang lifelessly against the trunk.

8 Squirt the palm leaf wires with hot glue and insert them into the hole at the top of the trunk. Hold for a few seconds until set, and arrange the leaves so that you have a full treetop.

9 Felt two COCONUT spheres out of dark brown roving about the size of marbles. Felt them to the palm tree where the trunk meets the leaves.

10 Optional: If your palm tree seems a little top heavy and wants to tip over, add a fun sandy base. Lightly sand the sharp edges of the circular wooden disk. Brush a thick coat of white craft glue all over the top of the disk and generously sprinkle sand all over it. Let the glue dry and shake off the excess sand; repeat the glue and sand process two or three more times for a solid coating. Once the sandy base is dry, just hot glue the wire bottom of the palm tree onto the center of the disk.

Sand Dollars

Sand dollars: the currency of the felt ocean. Give these critters a bit of color with a soft fabric paint wash.

Finished Size
4 inches (10.2 cm) in diameter

Materials & Tools
Templates (page 124)
Felting needle: 38 gauge
Foam felting mat
White wool craft felt
Core wool stuffing
Fabric paint in gray, tan, or yellow
Scissors
Small paintbrush

1. Trace and cut out two shells and one star shape from the white craft felt.

2. To create the **SHELL**, very lightly needle felt a tuft of core wool stuffing onto the center of one felt shell shape (fig. 1).

3. Place the second sand dollar on top of the first and begin to felt around the outside edge and the inside edges of the oval holes. Keep the felting within ¼ inch (.6 cm) of all the edges. Trim any fuzzy wool off the back of the sand dollar.

4. Lay the **STAR** shape over the sand dollar so that the points line up with the oval holes. Felt it in place by needle felting up the center of each arm of the star (fig. 2). A single line starting from the center and ending at each point will be enough to keep it in place.

5. Water down some gray or tan fabric paint. Use a small brush to add some shadows under the star shape and around the oval holes. Let the sand dollar air dry in the sun for a day.

FIGURE 1

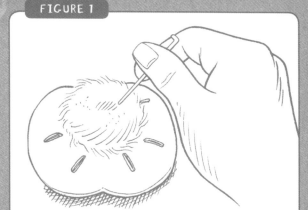

FIGURE 2

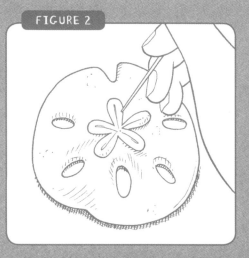

Starfish

Add as much—or as little—detail to your starfish as you like. The trick? Fabric paint and tufts of bright roving.

Finished Size
5 inches (12.7 cm) in diameter

Materials & Tools
Template (page 124)
Felting needle: 38 gauge
Foam felting mat
White craft felt
Core wool stuffing
Small tufts of orange, black, white, red, and yellow roving
Scissors
Fabric paint
1-inch (2.5 cm) sponge or bristle brush

1 Trace and cut out two **STAR** shapes from white craft felt. Very lightly needle felt tufts of core wool stuffing onto one side of one of the star shapes.

2 Sandwich the star shapes together and felt around the outside edges. Keep the felting within ¼ inch (.6 cm) of the edge. This will help puff out the middle of the star.

3 Starting at the center point on the back of the star, carefully cut a line up the center of each of the star's **ARMS** (fig. 1). Be careful to cut only through the one layer of white craft felt and the layer of core wool (but not the whole star). Felt down both sides of the cut line to create the gap that is seen on the undersides of starfish (fig. 2). Trim off any extra fuzzy wool that got poked through to the top of the starfish.

4 Shape the top of the starfish by felting down each side of the arms and focusing on the webbed areas between them. Felt the webbed area like an angled valley to help define obvious ridges on top of the star (fig. 3).

5 At this point you can either felt a yellow and orange wool layer over the top of the white felt, or use watered down fabric paint to get a blended color effect. If you choose fabric paint, dunk the whole starfish in water first to help the colors bleed together. Wring out the extra water so that the starfish is damp, not dripping. Start by dabbing the lightest colored paint on the outside edges with a sponge brush, and work darker colors in as you go towards the center. Add a little of the darkest color down the inside of the gap on the underside.

6 Let the starfish completely dry before adding any additional details. Tighten any sculpted areas that might have loosened while painting, and use tiny balls of colored wool roving rolled up with your fingers to needle felt in spots or highlight dots.

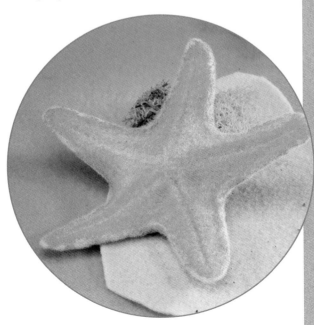

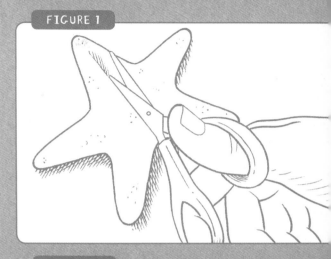

FIGURE 1

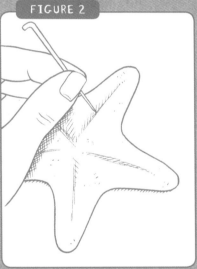

FIGURE 2

FIGURE 3

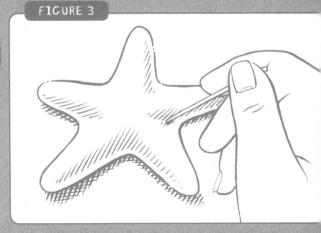

Pirate Map

With a yarn route to guide you, use this map to search out buried felt treasures!

Finished Size
9 x 7 inches (22.9 x 17.8 cm)

Materials & Tools
Diagram (page 125)
Felting needle: 38 gauge
Foam felting mat
White craft felt
Black wool yarn
Blue, red, brown, green, and yellow roving
Scissors
Fabric paint in brown and black
1-inch (2.5 cm) sponge brush or other paintbrush

1 Cut two identical rectangles of white craft felt that are a little smaller than a sheet of paper. Using the MAP diagram as a guide, draw your design onto one white craft felt rectangle.

2 Outline the IMAGES by felting black wool yarn around each element. Use the whole strand of black yarn to make thick bold lines, and use half of the strand to make thinner, more detailed lines. After the design is entirely outlined, start filling in the images by felting various wool roving colors. Use a bright blue for the OCEAN, a variety of greens to add depth to the PALM TREE, and bright red to help the X stand out.

3 Trim all the fuzzy wool off the back of the white craft felt. This will help create a nice thin piece when it's done.

4 Lay the finished map on top of the second piece of white craft felt. Felt the two pieces together by felting from the front and only in the white areas. Using sharp scissors, trim a jagged EDGE around the outside of the map.

5 After the map is securely felted together as one solid piece and the edges have been thoroughly distressed, dip the whole thing in a bowl of water and wring it out until it's damp, not dripping. This will help the fabric paint colors blend together and create an aged look.

6 Brush watered-down brown fabric paint around all the outer edges of the map. Be generous with the brown; when it dries it will fade as it bleeds in towards the center.

7 Sparingly brush concentrated black fabric paint onto the very outside edges. Allow the map to air dry.

Deck the
HALLS

'Tis always the season for felting. Set the mood with milk, cookies, your favorite holiday tunes, and felt yourself this merry little Christmas scene, featuring an elegant tree and a festive snowman.

Created by Cathy Gaubert

Christmas Tree

Give your felted version of this essential holiday fixture some frill with wraparound mini rickrack.

Finished Size
6 inches (15.2 cm) tall

Materials & Tools
Felting needles: 38 and 40 gauge
Foam felting mat
Green roving
Wool stuffing for core
Mini rickrack
Small pins or glue (optional)

1 Make a cone shape from the wool stuffing to create the core of the tree, needle felting it until it is slightly firm and measures approximately 6 inches (15.2 cm) tall with a 2½-inch (6.4 cm) base.

2 Starting at the bottom of the cone, wrap tufts of green roving around the core to cover it and needle felt the roving in place. Continue until the entire cone is covered. Turn the tree over, and do the same for the base.

3 Wrap a length of mini rickrack around the tree, beginning at the top and continuing until the bottom. Pin or glue in place.

Gifts

Squirt gun? Paint set? Who knows what's inside these pretty turquoise packages, all wrapped up with a bow!

Finished Size
1-inch (2.5 cm) square (largest)

Materials & Tools
Felting needles: 38 and 40 gauge
Foam felting mat
Upholstery foam (optional)
Scissors
Turquoise and light blue roving
Baker's twine

1 Cut upholstery foam into a 1-inch (2.5 cm) cube. Wrap small tufts of turquoise roving around the sides and begin needle felting them in place (fig. 1). Continue until all sides are covered.

2 If you want to skip the foam cube base, pull a tuft of turquoise roving, about 2 x 3 inches (5.1 x 7.6 cm), and roll it into a loose ball. Begin needle felting in the middle of the ball, moving out from the center in a squarish pattern. Turn over and repeat. Stand the shape on its end and continue needle felting it into a square shape. Turn over and repeat. Needle felt along the edges to continue shaping it into a cube.

3 Wrap baker's twine around the gift and tie.

4 Make more gifts in varying sizes. Flatten some out to make them more rectangular so that you can stack them up near the tree.

FIGURE 1

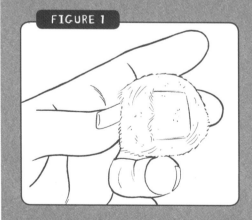

Teddy Bear

This cuddly Christmas companion is ready for action.

1 With a 2 x 2-inch (5.1 x 5.1 cm) tuft of brown roving, form a ball and needle felt to approximately ½ inch (1.3 cm) in diameter to form the **HEAD**.

2 With another tuft of brown roving (approximately the same size), needle felt the **BODY** into a 1-inch-tall (2.5 cm) cylinder (fig. 1). Stack the head and body and gently needle felt to join the two pieces.

3 Roll a 2 x 1-inch (5.1 x 2.5 cm) tuft of brown roving into a rope. Hold the rope in your hand and gently felt in both ends. Needle felt to approximately 1½ inches (3.8 cm) long, and then cut in the middle to make two **ARMS**. Make the **LEGS** in the same manner, but slightly thicker and longer.

4 Gently needle felt the arms and legs to the body (fig. 2).

FIGURE 1

FIGURE 2

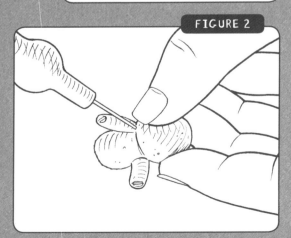

I've been a good bear this year.

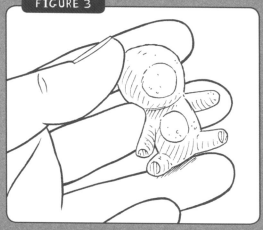

FIGURE 3

FIGURE 4

5 Needle felt tiny tufts of tan roving onto the teddy's **BELLY** and **MUZZLE** (fig. 3).

6 Roll two tiny tufts of black roving into small balls for the **EYES**. Gently needle felt them onto each side of the head, right above the muzzle.

7 For the **NOSE**, roll a small tuft of black roving into a ball and needle felt it onto the muzzle.

8 Roll two small tufts of brown roving into ball shapes (approximately ½ inch [1.3 cm]) for the **EARS**. At this point, you may want to pin the teddy to your foam work surface. Carefully needle felt the ears in place (fig. 4).

9 Once the ears are secured, needle felt a teeny bit of pink roving to the inside of each ear.

Snowman

Making this snowman in felt is just like making him in snow! Don't forget to add a carrot nose and, in the great tradition of Frosty, coal eyes.

Finished Size
2½ inches (6.4 cm) tall

Materials & Tools
Felting needles: 38 and 40 gauge
Foam felting mat
Orange, red, white, and black roving

1 With a 2 x 4-inch (5.1 x 10.2 cm) tuft of white roving, form a ball and needle felt to approximately 1¼ inches (3.2 cm) in diameter to begin forming the **BODY**. With a 2 x 3-inch (5.1 x 7.6 cm) tuft of white roving, needle felt a second ball to approximately 1 inch (2.5 cm) in diameter. With a 2 x 2-inch (5.1 x 5.1 cm) tuft of white roving, needle felt a third ball to approximately ¾ inch (1.9 cm) in diameter to form the **HEAD**.

2 Stack the middle ball on top of the base. Wrap a thin tuft of white roving around the middle where the two balls join. Needle felt to secure. Attach the head to the stack in the same manner.

3 Roll two teeny tufts of black roving into small balls for the **EYES**. Gently felt an eye onto each side of the head.

4 Roll a small tuft of orange roving for the **NOSE**, tapering the tip as you needle felt it. Needle felt it to the face.

5 With a two teeny tufts of red, felt a **HEART** onto the snowman's chest.

Stocking

Nothing says cozy like a stocking by the fireplace. Make yours with little bits of red and white roving.

Finished Size
2 inches (5.1 cm) tall

Materials & Tools
Felting needles: 38 and 40 gauge
Foam felting mat
Red and white roving
Sewing needle
Red thread

1 Roll a tuft of red roving into a 2¼-inch-long (5.7 cm) cylinder and gently needle felt, taking care to felt in the top end. For the **TOE** of the stocking, needle felt the end into a tapered shape.

2 Bend the stocking where the **HEEL** would be and needle felt around the bend so that the stocking holds its shape. You may need to add a bit more roving here to build up the heel.

3 Add small tufts of white roving to the toe and needle felt in place. Do the same with the heel of the stocking.

4 Thread a needle with a short length of red thread and knot both ends together, forming a loop to hang the stocking (by the chimney with care, perhaps!).

Mix-n-Match SCENES

If you could have only 3 things on a deserted island…

I wanna be in the circus, too!

yummy

nom, nom, nom…

What really lives in the woods. Or at least visits…

peekaboo!

My presents! MINE!

What happens when you mix these two chemicals?

A relaxing day in the park.

PARTY TIME!

Oh, look honey! Can we take one home?

Revenge of the dinosaurs.

Sewing is like a science, right?

Templates

All templates are at 100%.

Crab

Claw
cut 4

Leg
cut 6

Thumb
cut 2

Flappy Fin
cut 2

Starfish

cut 2

cut 2

Sand Dollar

cut 1

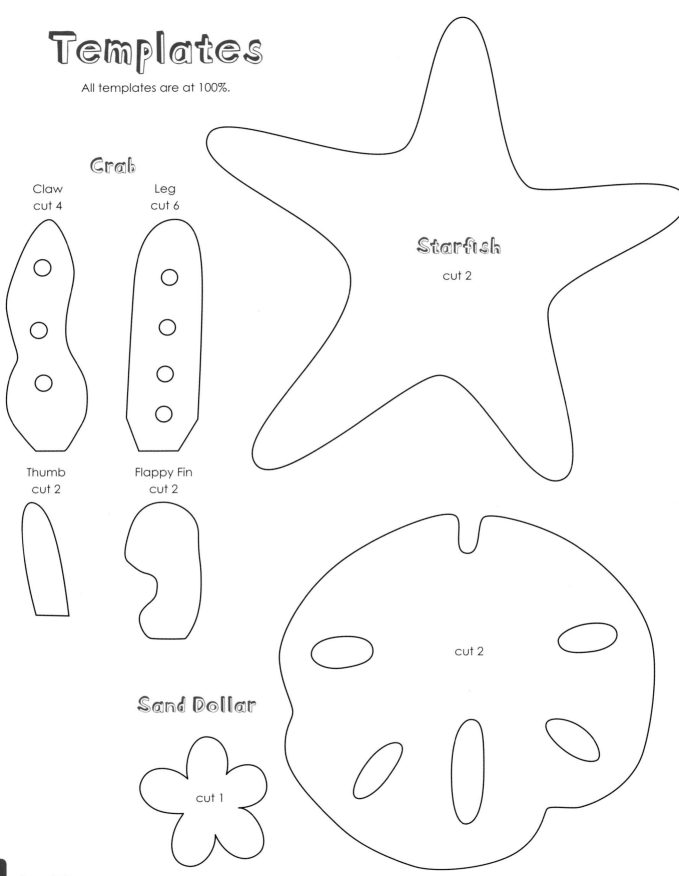

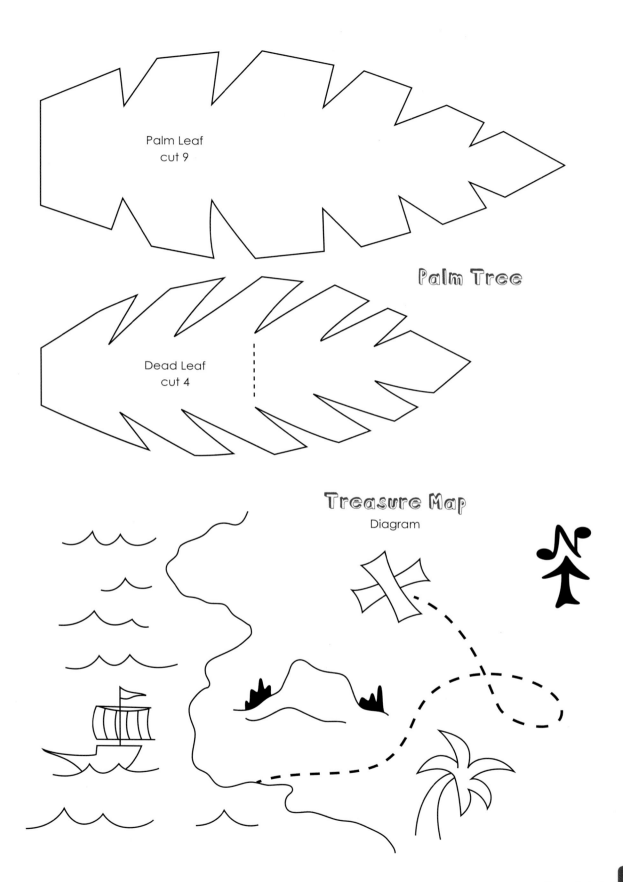

Palm Leaf
cut 9

Palm Tree

Dead Leaf
cut 4

Treasure Map
Diagram

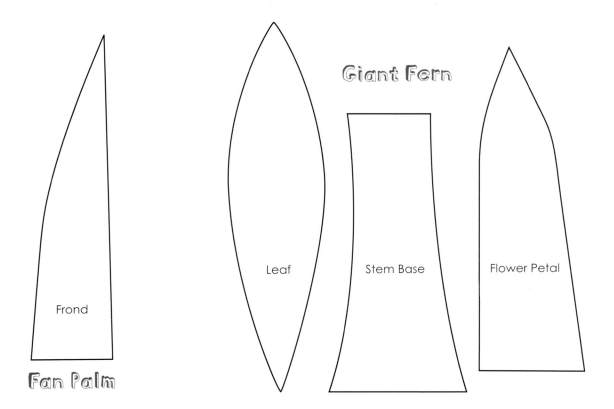

Fan Palm

Frond

Giant Fern

Leaf

Stem Base

Flower Petal

Teeth Pattern

T-Rex

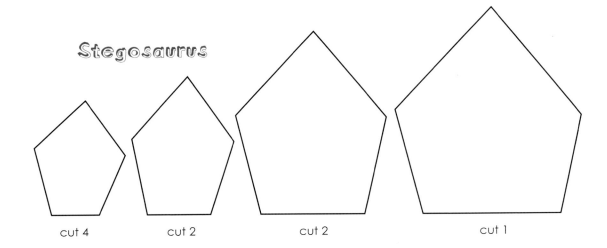

Stegosaurus

cut 4

cut 2

cut 2

cut 1

Carnivorous Plant

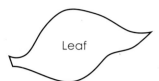

Leaf

Rocket Ship

Fin

Wooly Woodland

Stump Template and Stitching Pattern

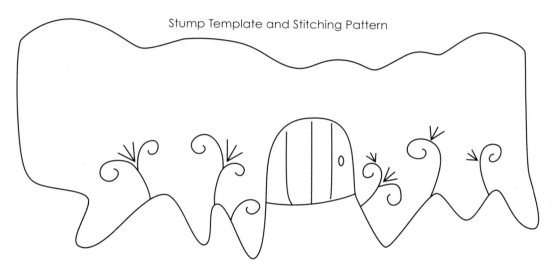

Base Template and Stitching Pattern

About the Designers

The creator of Sweet Felts, Yin Chan had been a handcrafter of various disciplines—knitting and paper arts to theatrical set design—before she was introduced to the unique art form and technique of needle felting. She uses her needle-felting skill to create sweet treat sculptures that are not only a delight to the eye but also can be handled and played with. When she's not poking away with her needles, she can be found in the kitchen creating various sweets to share with friends and family. You can also find her at sweetfelts.blogspot.com where she shares her pure wool sculptures with people who love sweets as much as she does.

Jenn Docherty is the author of the book *Sweet Needle Felts* and the creator of wee little needle felted creatures that she sells on her website, jenndocherty. com. She first started needle felting eight years ago, when she decided she'd rather not sew a bear in the traditional fashion, but try something new. That little pink teddy bear was the first of hundreds! She lives in an old house in New Jersey with her two little girls, her husband, one fat cat, and an overgrown garden.

Cathy Gaubert is a wife, momma, maker of things, author of *Pretty in Patchwork: Doll Quilts*, and contributor to many books from Lark Crafts. Her days are filled with the antics of three sweet girlies, and her kitchen table is filled with more works in progress than you can shake a stick at. Peer into her world at handmadecathygaubert.blogspot.com, and do be sure to say hello.

Michelle Kiker is a fiber artist, maker of things, and reader of books, currently living just outside of Philadelphia, Pennsylvania. A cuteness connoisseur, comic enthusiast, and explorer of everything awesome and fun, she takes inspiration from pop culture, nature, travel, and everyday objects. Michelle started needle felting in 2009 and has been creatively stabbing at wool roving ever since, bringing a menagerie of cute felted characters to life in her own unique, simple style. When not making felties, she can be found dabbling in watercolors, taking photo walks, or just generally trying to keep her cat and corgi from controlling the world. Check out more of her felted friends and daily life by visiting her website, Another No Mail Day, at nomailday.blogspot.com!

After getting her BFA at the Maryland Institute College of Art in Baltimore, Maryland, Chrissy Mahuna moved out to Hollywood to work in the entertainment industry. For the past seven years, she's been working as a scenic sculptor on projects ranging from big budget movies like *Land of the Lost* (which she met her husband on) and *Star Trek 2*, to theme-park rides like Disneyland's *Finding Nemo* and *Little Mermaid*, to large musical stage shows for performers such as Katy Perry, The Rolling Stones, and Cirque du Soleil. In addition to her professional sculpting, she has been working and selling felted sculptures since 2008, going by the alias *The Felted Chicken*. Working with wool is the perfect medium for her because she loves the playful nature of the final pieces, the soft and fluffy texture of the wool, and the fact that she can sculpt stuffed animals (since she's so bad at sewing)!

Heide Murray grew up in Canada and Maryland, but moved to Colorado for college and loves it there because her hair is not frizzy. Heide has been needle felting since 2001, after she went looking for a way to make her art dolls furry. Well, she never went back to making art dolls at all. The wonderful wool just never let go. Heide was a florist before having two daughters. Now she stays home (thanks, husband!) and makes lots of felted goodness for the world to see with her business, All Good Wishes. She has been teaching felting since 2006 and wishes she could see everyone's face when they make their first needle felted creature.

Aimee Ray has been making things from paper, fabric, and clay for as long as she can remember. She has a head full of ideas and is always working on something new. She is the author of *Doodle-Stitching*, *Doodle Stitching: The Motif Collection*, and *Doodle Stitching: Embroidery & Beyond*, and has contributed to many other Lark Crafts titles. You can see more of her work at dreamfollow.com.

Index